MW01228985

SOARING BEYOND FEAR

How to Overcome
Your Self-Imposed Limits...

Perry Chinn, D.C.

Soaring Beyond Fear

How to Overcome Your Self-Imposed Limits...

Address all inquiries to:

Dr. Perry Chinn

13028 Interurban S., #106

Seattle, WA 98168

Phone: 1-253-670-0858

www.SoaringBeyondFear.com

ISBN 978-1-93558602-9

Library of Congress Control Number: 2009913988

Editor: Tyler R. Tichelaar, Ph.D.

Cover Design: Shelly Batcher

Interior Layout: Fusion Creative Works, www.fusioncw.com

Printed in the United States of America

For additional copies, visit: www.SoaringBeyondFear.com

DISCLAIMER

Although this book is based on true events, all names, places, and events have been fictionalized, modified or changed completely to protect the innocent and the guilty, without implying either. Characters, institutions, corporations, and organizations are either products of the imagination or, if real, used fictitiously without any intent to describe their actual conduct, thoughts, physical characteristics, intentions, backgrounds, or medical conditions. Any similarity to actual people, events, or location is not intentional.

This book is solely intended for educational purposes. Any medical description or what may appear to be medical advice is not meant to be represented as accurate, safe, or, in some cases, even remotely possible. If you need medical or psychological care, please seek the help of a competent health care practitioner. It is never safe to self-diagnose. Any recommendations are the personal opinion of the author.

DEDICATION

To FB (aka Melanie), my beautiful wife, life partner, and friend. Thank you for being such a persistent teacher and coach. Your smile lights up my life and gives me the courage to continue to unravel this crazy experience called life.

To my kids, Brandon, Dylan, Jared, Colin, Katie, Andrea and Lindsey, AND our beautiful new granddaughter Leanora Hartley Poe, thank you for teaching me what unconditional love is all about.

To Mom and Dad. Thank you for being there and giving me this awesome opportunity to experience and express. And to my brothers and sisters for sharing my journey.

To my friend and coach, Bob Trask. You have helped me realize I do indeed have a purpose here on planet earth.

To Dr. Roger Turner, for your huge smile, even larger heart, and for opening my "mind."

To Jackson Tse, for helping to stretch me beyond my self-imposed limits.

To Stephanie Robinson, my tireless assistant and right arm. She continues to remind me of the virtue of the old saying, "You can catch more flies with honey than with vinegar."

To my readers—consciousness is indeed a gift like a sharp sword. Wield it wisely my friends!

ACKNOWLEDGMENTS

The sum of my life experience to this point is a result of the contributions of hundreds, probably thousands of people. Those whom I can best identify as having the greatest impact on me are:

Melanie Lee Vizzutti Chinn, Michael Failla, Charles Greene, Marilyn Gregg, Wayne E. Gustafson, Rod and Linda Handly, David Haynes, Esther and Jerry Hicks, George and Barb Hughes, Steven C. Knox, Marvin Kunikyo, Henry Madalian, Jean Templeton Morris, Don Mundy, Ken Nash, Ron Oberstein, Eric Plasker, Mark Rademacher, Leo Romero, Bruce Sprague, Charmi Sprague, Clyde Sprague, Steve Smith, Patrick Snow, Peter Stadelman, Eckhart Tolle, Jackson Tse, Bob Trask, Roger Turner, and David Warwick.

CONTENTS

Introduction   11

Section 1: Ignorance is Bliss   **17**

Chapter 1: Sleeping Peacefully   19

Chapter 2: Leaving the Tribe—Identifying Family   47

Chapter 3: Surviving the Pain of Separation: I Leave
My Church Family   57

Chapter 4: Seeking Salvation   77

Section 2: The Voice   **87**

Chapter 5: Discovering Chester   89

Chapter 6: Taming Chester   113

Chapter 7: Observing Chester   147

Chapter 8: Leaving Fear Behind   163

Section 3: Accountability   **191**

Chapter 9: Rising Above the Victim Identity   193

Chapter 10: Nurturing Spirit   201

Chapter 11: Learning about Risk   233

Chapter 12: Fear and Separation: Breaking Down Walls   241

Chapter 13: The World and Fear   263

Section 4: Vision   **277**

Chapter 14: Living Beyond Fear   279

Chapter 15: Soaring In Joy   293

Recommended Reading   299

About the Author   303

INTRODUCTION

"Only when we are no longer afraid do we begin to live."
— **Dorothy Thompson**

I am no longer content to live in fear. Next year I will be fifty years old, and I don't want to spend one more day ruled and paralyzed by the fear-mind. Fear has infected the consciousness of virtually every inhabitant of this planet to one degree or another, and the inevitable result has been the draining of joy from the lives of countless millions.

This book is an attempt to share with you, the reader, my experience in understanding and moving through the paralysis of fear. My personal journey has taken most of my lifetime, and it is not over yet. I have so much more to learn and experience just like you. My wish is that the unnecessary suffering accompanying this journey of discovery will not consume the majority of your life as well. Life, at least in this physical experience, is indeed short. It is far too brief and precious to waste on anything less than full joy and consciousness, unless of course that path is your intentional choice.

Look around you. It is very easy to observe that almost all the people we interact with as we go through our days are controlled by fear or their lives are in some way repressed by fear.

My goal with this book is humbly to enlighten and assist you in waking up to who you are. You are not the fear that consumes your thought. The really incredible thing is that all you are and need to know is right there, inside you. I am not able to *give* you anything of substance. The only gift I can give is possibly to be an agent causing a brief opening of understanding. The "Aha!" that cuts like a knife through the fog of fear.

I have no way of knowing exactly where you are on the path of spiritual awakening, your return to knowing whom you are. In fact, you may be light years ahead of me! If so, I am honored to share this journey with you, and I look forward with joyful expectation to meeting you, hearing your story, and reading your book!

During my first meeting with my publishing coach, Patrick Snow, regarding this book, he asked me a very specific question, "Why are you writing your book?" My immediate answer was that I envisioned the publishing of my book serving as a platform in which to speak, an opportunity to share my experience with others. My wife would agree that I love to talk. A talent of mine, one that at times greatly embarrasses her, is that I can strike up a conversation with a total stranger and within minutes create a relationship that can last for years.

One of the most fulfilling and exciting weekends of my life was spent in the hills of California assisting my friend Bob Trask in giving a men's spiritual retreat. The setting was in the incredibly beautiful foothills of the California Sierras. One afternoon after a session, as Bob and I walked through a meadow during one of the breaks, we noticed a hawk soaring silently just over our heads. We both looked up and observed the graceful flight of this magnificent animal and smiled at the synchronicity of our shared totem leading us on our walk. I was exhilarated by the morning's experience, and I shared with Bob that I felt this work was what I was meant to do. I was born to fly, to soar, to share, to teach, and to instruct. My diversion into the world of helicopter instruction is but a pale metaphor, exciting as it is, for my real purpose here on earth.

When I see the excitement and the flicker of understanding come alive in the eye of another life traveler, it gives me chill bumps. Nothing is greater to experience in my opinion. As we are all sojourners in this experience called Life, I view my job as helping others pull themselves out of the ditch of unconsciousness and back onto the road of awareness.

A common misconception in the world is that the thinking mind is king. The Descartes quotation, "I think; therefore, I am" is often stated as some wise, philosophical truth. We acknowledge and revere scientists for their amazing abilities to innovate and discover. Granted, mankind has made incredible progress in science and technology. No one can argue that fact. However, it is also true that the mind, the ego-identified thinking mind, or what I like to call the "fear-mind," has tremendous limitations. It can only go so far in helping us understand who we are and why we exist.

In fact, this fear-mind can actually be our greatest challenge. What may scientifically be a tremendous asset could in fact be the biggest roadblock in our spiritual journey.

When we make the mistake of identifying with our fear-mind, the problems begin to arise. When we are ruled by fear, the thinking, problem-solving mind can cripple and obscure the light of our spiritual consciousness.

This book contains four sections that outline the process of one man's journey toward awareness and conquering the crippling effects of fear. I am not saying I have arrived, or that I have achieved any level of wisdom or consciousness unavailable to the next man. In fact, just ask any of my friends how Buddha-like I am at times. They will probably get a big kick out of letting you know how "unenlightened" I can be. This book is written from my perspective, assisted by the teachings of hundreds of authors and teachers of many varied philosophies and disciplines. You may not resonate with all the messages here, but you will resonate with the messages you are meant to hear and see. As none of us are created exactly the same in this life, we all must arrive at our assigned goals of understanding in our own time. Just as no leaf or snowflake is exactly alike, though they do share the same basic blueprint, our path to realization will be unique.

I am confident you will find what you are looking for to improve your life. It may not be contained in the pages of this book; however, I firmly believe, at the appropriate time, your specific life lesson will reveal itself. This book may be the stepping-stone to the next book or teacher with the very words that trigger your personal "Aha!" When you feel the pain of a challenged belief or threatened agreement, I encourage you to read on. Develop the courage to dig deep to the source of that pain and bring to light what is being challenged. The pain is present not to punish or judge you; it is created to help bring you back to understanding. And it is helpful to remember that no work is required here; it is more about allowing the process you have invited.

Lastly, know that like you, I am a humble traveler in this experience called life. You have drawn this book into your experience. There is no mistake there. Remember that you are the intentional creator of your experience. Acknowledge this truth and the job is mostly done.

This book is meant to stretch and challenge you. I will know whether I have done my job if this book pushes your buttons a bit. So please, read on....

Perry L. Chinn, D.C.

SECTION

1

IGNORANCE IS BLISS

1

SLEEPING PEACEFULLY

"It's not color, race, or even language that separates people. It is fear."
— **Perry L. Chinn, D.C.**

It has been said that ignorance is bliss. I would like to add that ignorance can also be very painful, and it can contribute to a great deal of misery.

From a very early age, I was deathly afraid of a short four-letter word beginning with the letter "f." Being raised as a good God-"fear"ing Seventh-day Adventist young man, I knew certain words were just not uttered, or even thought of for that matter. Yes, a couple of examples would fit this word description, but the word "fear" is by far the most common and potentially detrimental to the human race. And it can be particularly devastating to the individual unconsciously awash in mind-controlling fear.

It took me many years to figure out that most of my own life was lived in and controlled by fear. What seemed perfectly normal to me, because I had been raised with that awareness, was actually crippling my ability to engage in any real level of spiritual understanding. And to make matters worse, most people I associated with were also deeply mired in a coma of fear-motivated existence.

My sense of blame wanted to point the finger at those who had raised and nurtured me—my church, parents, and Sabbath School teachers. But when I took some time to examine the situation, I sadly realized they were no better off than me, having themselves been taught all their lives the same pattern of day-to-day duty and to live almost entirely motivated by fear.

I don't know why some people wake up to an understanding of this affliction while many more go to their graves blissfully unaware of any alternative to their fear-based existences. The only explanation that comes close to making sense to me is that we are each somehow responsible for creating the syllabus for this lesson and experience we call "life."

Somehow, I chose the advanced lesson from the school of hard knocks. The "spirituality for dummies" path of enlightenment. The dummy part meant I had to create a great deal of pain for myself to move me toward an awareness that the pain and suffering may not have been necessary. By observing others around me, I noted that some people seemed to coast serenely through life, calmly navigating the course of their personal events, while for some reason, I seemed to create a much more dramatic path.

Not that I am complaining! As a wise soul shared with me years ago, "You will know you have arrived at a measure of wisdom when you can look back over your years and be grateful for each event and each day of it." I am not too sure about the "wisdom" part of that statement; however, I can attest to the gratefulness. I am truly thankful for all I am and all I have been shown on this journey. Although much of it has not been easy, it has transpired much like any birth—discomfort was involved. And at times, it was messy.

From my limited observation of others, I believe reaching a mature level of personal accountability is a rare and precious achievement. To get there, all blame must be set aside. No other person is responsible for the place where I find myself today.

To me this level of responsibility is empowerment at its highest level! To realize I truly am the sole author and creator of my personal experience is a very rewarding epiphany!

But this realization took me many years to reach.

My earliest memories include playing in the muddy creek beds near my home in Spangle, Washington. This tiny town is still today far off the beaten track and actually a very good place for a young boy to spend his early years. Life consisted of going to school (you know, the walking several miles to school in three feet of snow, uphill both ways), then meeting up with my friend

Marty after class to explore the tiny town and surrounding wheat fields.

We raided the pea fields for ammunition for our peashooters. Marty and I made "forts" in the tall wheat, which necessitated our avoiding the farmers who, for some reason, had an issue with young boys trampling flat their nice billowing wheat.

The town had long straight hills for sledding in the winter and riding bikes in the summer. We had tremendous fun even without knowing what video games were.

We pulled pop bottles out of the mud to clean up and turned them in for the deposit refund. The nickels and dimes we collected gave us the buying power we needed for the life-sustaining candy and soda pop purchased at the local general store. Life was an adventure, and at the time, fear played a very small part. I can still close my eyes and smell the musty smell of the dry creek bottoms. Life was good.

But as I grew older, I began to see the effects of fear in my parents' lives. With five children, my parents perceived money as scarce, creating much fear about our lack of abundance. The consciousness of lack was prominent in our lives. Other kids had new shoes and the finest clothes. Other families drove shiny new cars while we seemed to get the older ones that broke down frequently and had flat tires at the most inopportune times.

I was learning about fear, and at the same time, I was taking on a belief system that I was meant to drift through life, subject to fate, luck, or God. I knew nothing about the ability to direct my life's path. I was learning to react and assume the role of the victim. It would take me many years to realize that deep within me was the spiritual seed that would eventually blossom into joy, knowing, and awareness.

Looking back on the events of my childhood, I can now see how I learned these things. And as I have learned to move through the judgment and blame, wonderful opportunities for growth have presented themselves. Where before I had learned to harbor resentment and blame, now I feel mostly empathy and a growing understanding.

It has taken me a longer time to get over the anger directed at my parents.

"They did the best they could." — **Unknown**

"I do the very best I know how—the very best I can; and mean to keep doing so until the end. If the end brings me out all right, what is said against me won't amount to anything." — **Abraham Lincoln**

Forgiveness. Without a doubt this has been my greatest personal challenge. It's easy to talk about, quite another thing to put into practice on a consistent basis. The act of forgiveness is okay for someone else to do, but me? I had so much invested in the pain and grudges accumulated over the years from all the perceived wrongs that had been "done to me." This was a burden I was not going to lay aside easily.

Historically, I tended to be a "black or white" kind of person. Things were either right or wrong. Truth or error. The shades of gray that many people seemed to understand often eluded me. But in my arrogance, born of ego, I, of course, thought myself blessed with the discernment to know the difference! And I tended to inform people of my advanced level of discernment at pretty much any available opportunity.

It turned out that the forgiveness lesson for me, when at long last I was willing to receive it, was pivotal in allowing my life to move forward.

As I entered adulthood and became responsible for myself and then responsible for my wife and children, I found there was a lot I did not know about life—a lot that could be considered basic survival skills. One of my main gripes was that no one had taught me about finances, relationships, or parenting. Up to this point, I had stumbled through life learning these lessons the hard way.

Learning financial responsibility by trial and error is not only costly, but in my experience, it tends to be downright painful! So with the financial pain accumulating, I began to harbor a serious collection of grudges for many years, far into my adult life. This was at great expense, I might add, to my level of joy, happiness, and business success.

As time moved on, I was convinced that my less than optimal success in relationships and business was not my fault! No one had taught me how to be successful! Someone or something outside of myself was obviously responsible for my misery. Since what I felt I should have learned I also felt should have been the responsibility of my parents, I directed my blame at them, seeing all their shortcomings and wondering how they could have failed me the way they did.

As I was struggling with the blame directed at my parents, my wife seemed to feel that if I could learn to forgive them for how I thought they had failed me and focus on what they did right, it would be instrumental in allowing me to continue on my path of personal growth.

I am slowly learning to listen to my wife, so I gave the forgiveness idea a try. And it turns out my wife was right! It was essential for me to arrive at the understanding that based on the awareness they had at the time, my parents really did do the best they could. And with great relief, I found that when I finally allowed myself to let the judgments go, the release was incredible.

The accountability lesson I had drawn into my experience gave me a growing feeling of empowerment. Gradually, I learned no one else is responsible for my misery, or my happiness for that matter.

> *"It is far better to forgive and forget than to*
> *hate and remember."* — **Unknown**

Non-forgiveness is the very nature of the fear-mind. I was totally identified with fear at this stage in my life, but fortunately, while others might allow themselves to become victims of fear,

I was destined to create my way out of it. At my then current level of consciousness, overcoming that fear would involve creating pain and conflict as I found my way to freedom from the fear. Eventually, I realized the purpose of this suffering was to motivate me through the fear consciousness.

To explain my fear consciousness, I need to explain a bit more about my family situation growing up. My earliest memories of my father are rather hazy and indistinct. He seemed to be away a lot, but at my young age, not knowing anything different, I perceived that as "normal." Other than some fond memories of camping trips to Yosemite, which led to a lifelong love for Nature and the outdoors, I don't remember spending much time with him. I know that he did spend time with me; however, my perception was that I was often left to discover life on my own.

Within six years of my birth, my older brother and I would adapt to sharing my parents with three more siblings and the Seventh-day Adventist Church. My father and mother were often busy with church meetings, choir practices, and obligations upon which I can only now speculate. Their day to day "busy-ness" seemed to consume their lives. As I witnessed other kids spending time with their dads, I began to resent my father, and feelings of loss grew into sorrow and then anger. My mother was working full-time from as early as I can remember to help support our family. In hindsight, I can understand her commitment to provide for us; however, at the time I only felt loneliness over my parents' absence. I later vowed never to neglect my own kids, no matter how busy I became in my adult life. Now that I am a father, my understanding of my parents' experience is greatly enhanced.

Today, I think the main problem is that neither of my parents was prepared to meet the demands of a large family. My father hadn't learned much about financial management when he was growing up, also due to lack of instruction from his parents on the subject. My dad always seemed to be in debt and struggling to meet his financial obligations. Stress over money matters was an ever-present fixture in our household from my earliest memories. As I grew up, a victim identity began to overtake my mind-set, making me believe I didn't stand a chance. I would have to learn about financial and spiritual abundance the hard way.

When collecting soda bottles from streambeds and roadsides no longer gave me the level of affluence I desired, I stumbled into the newspaper industry. Our town of two hundred and fifty people needed a local delivery boy and I had a bicycle! After a phone call and a short interview, I was in business!

I got up early in the morning to deliver the papers. I showed up, got the job done on a consistent basis, and even earned some bonuses. I remember the first bonus gift I received was a matching hatchet and knife set. At ten years of age, to own a real hunting knife and hatchet was a significant testament to my maturity. Today, I realize it was just a couple of pieces of stamped metal with plastic handles, but at the time, I thought it a real achievement. I remember strapping on my knife and hatchet and heading out into the wilderness with pride.

I kept my paper route for about a year until my father was transferred to a new job and we moved across the state to the Seattle area. Once we were settled in southeast King County, I was fortunate to make friends with a young man whose father was a logger. My education concerning the value of hard work and responsibility was about to begin.

Developing My Work Ethic

Finding myself once again in a new school, I struggled to fit in. Being a bit on the chunky side and having higher-than-average book skills, I was often persecuted and rather self-conscious as a result. My desire to fit in and be accepted was very powerful. But it was nothing compared to my desire to "be good" and please God.

One of my classmates, Bruce, presented me with the opportunity to stretch my wings a little. Bruce's parents were a logger and a stay-at-home mom. By comparison, my own mother had worked as long as I could remember, often leaving us kids to fend for ourselves after school, including long waits for a ride home.

Bruce introduced me to BB guns, knives (I still feel great remorse for the less fortunate creatures we were able to catch or shoot), Coca-Cola, and fireworks. He also taught me (along with his father Clyde), in a not too gentle manner, the value of working hard and long.

Loggers have always been a tough breed. Just like in baseball, in the woods, there's no crying. Hard work was the primary virtue, and softer skills such as a college education were typically scorned and mocked. Days began early—the goal was to be on the job site before the sun rose. Slim profit margins, equipment maintenance issues, and fire danger restrictions in summer necessitated working hard and fast while you could.

Despite these difficulties, Clyde was a fair and honest man. If anything, obstacles only caused him to work harder and smarter. Like his son Bruce, he had very little empathy for sore muscles and the "I can't" attitude; in fact, I am sure those words never entered either's consciousness. It was not "No way" but rather, "Give me a minute to think and I will make the way" and they did—usually with a bulldozer or other piece of heavy equipment.

When Bruce and I were about twelve, I remember Clyde coming down from the woods one day with a pickup piled high with straight-grained old-growth cedar. I can still smell the sweet pungency of the wood when I close my eyes today. Handing Bruce a fro and mallet, he showed his son the art of splitting the thin boards into "shakes," the material for roofing so prized at the time across the country. Very soon I was offered the chance to share in the work (and the profits) of this new business venture.

We soon graduated to a hay-baler, a crudely jury-rigged contraption originally designed to harvest grass. The piston that would have pushed out a hay bale was used to shove a bolt of fine-grained cedar into a sharp knife. As the shake (shingle) split away from the bolt, the piston returned to ready for another cycle of splitting the shakes. Trimmed and bundled, the shakes were ready for the roofer to nail or staple to the roof for a watertight and very attractive roof.

At sixteen, Bruce made a very daring business move. I can still recall the day we drove to Jackson Street in Seattle and looked at and loaded up the shining new hydraulic splitter and nine foot tall bandsaw. The profits as well as the dangers soared. Somehow, I was able to hang on to all ten of my fingers, a feat especially remarkable and fortunate considering my current profession as a chiropractor. I recall visiting shake mills, places that looked more condemned than not, manned by old men of all ages with 100 proof blood coursing through their veins. I was impressed that they had any appendages below their elbows.

The work was hard, but I was able to pay my way through private high school (as well as my sister's), buy a car and clothes, and learn for the first time the awesome independence a "man of means" had.

I divided my time between school, the shake mill, the woods when they needed an extra hand, and my girlfriend.

Clyde had his ups and downs in the lumber industry, particularly in the late '70s and early '80s as logging became a threat to the endangered spotted owl, and dwindling old growth supplies and foreign competition squeezed the profits to a stop. By the time an injury in the woods opened my eyes to the world of chiropractic, it was time to leave the logging industry world.

Bruce eventually diversified into the roofing installation business, still doing some cedar work but more and more of the asphalt shingle. Today he is one of the largest roofers in the northwest and still jokingly chides me for leaving "all of this." I don't think he has ever really understood my need to go on to college.

I will always be exceedingly grateful for the lessons Clyde and Bruce taught me. Their teaching methods were rough at times, but I really feel they always had my best interests at heart. As I watch my own four sons grow to manhood today, I see them struggle with the temptations of entitlement and ease and how difficult it can be to develop a hands-on understanding of work ethic.

While I value the work ethic I developed from these experiences, I also realize the danger of believing that abundance can only come from hard work. If we believe universal abundance only arrives through one vehicle, we can severely limit the opportunity to receive through other avenues.

In her book *You Can Heal Your Life*, Louise Hay taught me much about abundance and how our belief systems surrounding money and work can manifest themselves in our health. The following quote by Louise Hay has been very helpful to me:

"In the infinity of life where I am all is perfect, whole and complete…for I am a beloved child of the Universe, and the Universe lovingly takes care of me…"

There truly is no limit to the ability of our universal Source to provide for our experience here. We are complete; lack is an illusion perpetuated by the fear-mind primarily to justify its version of self, and of course, its very existence.

It can be a struggle to remember, but it's helpful to realize that if we are open to it, we can receive from a multitude of channels. Putting limits on abundance and sources of wealth frustrates the universe's ability to provide. Our fear-mind would prefer to keep our perspective limited and our receiving net closed up tight. "Life is hard and there is only so much to go around" is a commonly held belief system in our world. Instead, we can alternatively develop the ability to see how abundance can stream into our lives through thousands of different channels. Our job is to declare our intention and be open to the possibilities.

My first car was a tremendous learning experience for me. The process of putting my first car together taught me the value of doing things right the first time, which included envisioning and allowing for abundance to enter my life.

I was one of those kids in line at the department of motor vehicles to get my license on my sixteenth birthday. Today, young people seem to be much more laid-back about the process, waiting to get their licenses when the need arises, such as a job or girlfriend across town. But my desire to have my license was all about the sheer joy of freedom and the incredible FUN of driving! I couldn't wait to have that piece of paper officially declaring my right to burn gasoline and wear out tires.

The object of my automotive desire arrived in the form of a "fixer-upper." Of course, I was too green in the world of autos to know what that really meant; I was just excited to have a car! For many years, my uncle had been in the business of repairing damaged cars for re-sale, so he became the logical source for my first car.

The car turned out to be a 1973 Honda Civic, only three years old and in relatively good shape, at least on the outside. The only problem was that the engine would not turn over. Even though I couldn't start the engine, I remember the thrill of sitting in the driver's seat and dreaming about driving down the long roads. Since the engine didn't work, it was indeed a dream. But I had the vision!

My dad and I towed my car the long two hundred and fifty miles back to our house. Once home, I wasted very little time wrestling the oil pan off, my first journey into major auto surgery. And there it was—a thrown connecting rod. It would be a major repair, but at least now I knew what the problem was. Since the car needed a complete engine rebuild, the repair costs would start accumulating fast, and because it was my project and funds were tight, I knew I would have to rebuild the motor myself. After my dad helped me pull out the engine and take it apart, we carefully put all the little parts in cans and plastic bags for a hopefully uneventful re-build.

A few days later, my hand trembled as I wrote the one hundred and twenty dollar check for a new crankshaft. I thought it must be made of solid gold to cost that much, but it sure looked beautiful lying there in its cardboard packing box. A few more weeks and several trips to the Honda dealer later, I was ready to start the engine! And the extra parts box only had a few bolts and springs in it! Amazing! Obviously, the engine didn't need all those extra parts....

I suppose a romantic end to this story would be a problem free first car experience. It was anything but. However, what I did learn was perseverance and quite a lot about the power of vision. With each nut and bolt I fastened, I could see and remember the touch and smell of my first sight of the little Civic, but most importantly, I envisioned the car moving under its own power. Eventually, the happy day came when I turned the key in the ignition, the engine started up, and I pulled out of the driveway onto the road.

That little car would take me thousands of miles, take my girlfriend and me on our first date, and be the stepping-stone for my next auto adventure. My appreciation for my little brown car was largely due to my tearing it apart and putting it back together. That process made her mine. I still have a soft spot for that little brown Honda today. Now where did I put those pictures?

With the years, I have come to appreciate all the new challenges I unendingly create. Some are fun, while some definitely belong in the four-letter word category, but all provide me with invaluable learning experiences. Vision, intention, and expectation—that is the recipe for creation. The taste of goal realization will fall flat if any of these ingredients are left out.

One of my challenges today is constantly to guard myself against making my kids' lives too "easy." In order to grow strong spiritually and emotionally, they must create their own paths and experiences and be rewarded accordingly. The process itself is so very valuable. Removing the challenge of life from those we care about is often crippling rather than helpful. So I must remind myself each day to let my children create and experience the joy of their own lives. Any assistance given must be for the purpose of helping them build their strength and confidence; we cannot build these for them.

You too have your own "little brown car" story. Have you shared it lately? Each one of us has a unique experience that can make a difference in the life of another struggling to stay ahead of his or her fear-mind. No one has your story. So please share it.

My success with my car set me on my journey to wake out of my dream of fear and lack of confidence. The journey would introduce me to many different people and experiences, each with a valuable lesson for me.

Another major step on that journey to awakening happened several years later. I had married and was still working with Bruce and Clyde when I nearly lost my life.

We were "switching roads" one day, a process that involves moving very large cables, thousands of feet long, to a new position on the hill. This new orientation of line allows for access of a new swath, or "road" of logs to be dragged down the hill by the yarder. The yarder is a huge machine, weighing about 100 tons, which has a tall tower with cables stretching down, or up, the hill being harvested. The powerful diesel engine turns big drums of line, which pull the logs to the landing area for loading on the trucks.

That day, the boss and I were up on the steep hillside "choking" logs for the yarder to pull to the landing. I remember it was a warm day, the sun was shining, and there was lots of work to do. During the process of switching the lines around, a line often would snag or become caught on a log, stump, or other obstruction. When this happened, we would signal the yarder engineer to stretch all the lines taut with the intention of clearing any snags.

Of course, whenever we signaled for movement of lines or logs, we would get well out of the way. This process was no different on that day, though maybe the boss was being a little confident. At any rate, as the lines grew taut, a long log way up the hill caught the cable and was dislodged from its resting place. Instead of rolling down the hill, it came shooting down the slope more like a toboggan on steroids. Clyde, the boss, hollered and we both started running for a stump to hide behind. To this day I am not sure why I stopped to look, but the next thing I remember is lying face down in the dirt with the feel and sound of a freight train rumbling over the top of my tin safety hat. The split second it took seemed more like half an hour!

Jim, the yarder operator, shared with me later that he watched in horror and "knew" I must be dead. No one could survive an impact like that. His feeling of helplessness, having no control over the log, being almost a half-mile away, was frightening.

Now I am not sure what form our guardian angels take; what I do know is that mine was definitely on duty that day! Clyde, by that time aware that I had not followed him to the stump, witnessed the tail end of my tangle with the eighty-foot tree and hurried over to see what piece of me was left. I am sure he had visions of state inspectors, skyrocketing insurance premiums, and an irate widow in his mind, which were relieved only when he saw I was still alive. Not only alive, but after a few minutes of rest, I took advantage of the adrenaline created and went back to work.

Of course, I did the macho thing that evening and told my wife I had scratched my face after work playing basketball with the guys. She was more than a little miffed when I confessed the true story a few days later.

That event, however, led to the end of my manual labor in the woods. While valuable and life-long lessons had been learned there, it was now time for me to explore more of what life had to offer. The injuries, minor though they seemed at the time, eventually landed me in a chiropractor's office where I discovered a whole new world. You mean I can work inside in a clean shirt, still work with my hands, help people, and make good money? Sign me up!

With my passion and purpose strong, in the fall of 1983 I enrolled at Life Chiropractic College in Marietta, Georgia. My wife was a bit shocked with my exuberant and sudden decision to move from Seattle to Atlanta to go to chiropractic school. We had to pass about a dozen other chiropractic institutions on our way there; however, my chiropractor, Dr. Les, assured me that this was by far the best school to attend. I went there to learn chiropractic, little guessing I would also be exposed to what at the time was considered "New Age consciousness." The move would put me way outside my comfort zone, emotionally, geographically, and spiritually.

Raised from birth as a Seventh-day Adventist, I had been instilled with a healthy fear of anything non-biblical (anything non-Adventist for that matter). And when I say biblical, I mean Biblical! Adventists have historically prided themselves upon their literal and Holy Spirit inspired interpretation of not only the New Testament, but the Old as well. The teaching inferred that we were to be suspicious of those who did not believe the way we did.

I grew up singing songs about Jesus and "happy, happy homes," learning early that happiness here on earth and then in Heaven depended on how well you knew the Bible, kept its rules and knew its Author.

I was typically the one in the front row, singing the loudest, always knowing my assigned memory verse and being on time for Sabbath School class. I was learning early on that being accepted by my church family was to be a central tenet in my personal value system.

As an adult, I was then the one teaching the Bible lessons to the younger kids. I sang in the choir and helped build the new church building in the mid '70s. After graduating from chiropractic college and returning to my home church, I would be selected to be a church elder, an honor more due to my professional status than any wisdom attained at such a young age. I would serve in many capacities in the church including school board chairman and church board member. I was working hard at being a "good" guy.

I was still a card-carrying conservative Christian when my wife and I arrived in Marietta, Georgia to take on this new chiropractic career. It was a rainy day when our small caravan rolled into town. The sky was crying and so was my wife, neither of us having ever been further east than Colorado. First, we visited the apartments recommended by the student services department. What a shock! The colorful, inviting photos of student housing were a classic case of bait and switch. Even though we had both been raised in fairly humble surroundings, my wife refused to live in such squalor. So we found an inexpensive motel for the night.

The next day, our second stop in this new and strange southern town was the local Seventh-day Adventist church. Here at least was family, right? No one was there on that mid-week day except an older gentleman working on the lawn. He turned out to be about as friendly as a water moccasin, an attribute that did little to cheer up my wife or lift my spirits. We mentioned we were new in town and I would be attending the chiropractic college. I was hopeful the doors of hospitality would be thrown open, but I was sadly mistaken. We would later befriend a wonderful couple in the church who agreed that this gentleman was best not nominated for the welcoming committee.

Eventually, we found a suitable and inexpensive two-bedroom apartment in Smyrna, a town a few miles south of Marietta. It didn't take long to move our things from the small U-haul trailer into the apartment, and we soon settled into school life. I immediately met new people at Life University, quickly building friendships that have lasted to this day. My wife had it a bit harder as she headed out into a strange new world to find employment to help support us while I went to school. Since both of us came from solid southern Idaho stock, we did okay, even though the first few months were tough.

I knew I was on the right track. The inspiration of my old friend, Dr. Les, had helped to guide me to what I was convinced was a life of prosperity and purpose. What little I knew of chiropractic philosophy at the time had attracted me to the people and students at Life. The next four years were challenging, yes, but they also provided a level of support I haven't quite felt since. I had plugged into the web of Life, and my tenuous grasp felt an attractive energy that pulled me in. I am filled with gratitude to this day.

One of the first people I met at Life University was Steve, a young man from Arkansas, by way of California. Steve quickly let me know that he was quite familiar with this new culture and life philosophy called chiropractic, having spent the last few years as business manager for a multi-clinic chiropractic corporation in San Francisco. This news quickly moved him to the top of our class list of people "in the know," a position he comfortably took on.

Some of our classmates saw Steve as a bit pretentious and obnoxious, but my wife and I found Steve and his wife Mary to be intriguing. We were soon invited over for dinner and introduced to their way of looking at life and Spirit. They had a new baby boy and seemed to have a worldly sophistication that was both attractive and at the same time a bit scary. They introduced us to some new concepts in nutrition and some other ideas and views that were not necessarily compatible with our conservative religious upbringing. I found that my belief systems, inside and outside the classroom, were being challenged on a daily basis.

The next few years were full of new experiences, and Steve and I gradually became good friends. We spent hundreds of hours studying for tests and board exams, and the five of us explored the mountains of north Georgia together, shared many meals, and experienced the ups and downs of college life. My time at Life flew by and I was soon to graduate as a new chiropractor.

Soon after graduation, Steve and Mary separated and divorced, a very difficult time for both of them and for their young son. I remember Steve later attributing the breakup to

Mary's liaison with a "New Age" minister she had met at a retreat in California.

I didn't hear much from Steve for over a year. I worried and thought about him frequently during this time until I ran into him at a seminar in Wisconsin. He was finally ready to reconnect with me. Over pizza after the seminar meeting, he shared his experience and told the story of his new friendship with a former classmate of ours whom he would eventually marry. The real piece of news, and quite a shocker for me, was that he had become a born again Christian "again." And a quite zealous "born again" Christian at that. I was very surprised that he could move from what I viewed as a very open-minded spiritual philosophy back to a more structured and seemingly restrictive religious belief system. But for Steve, the pendulum had swung too hard in the opposite direction in the previous chapter of life, and he apparently attributed the "anything goes'" and "do it if it feels good" philosophy he had experienced in the "New Age" world to the traumatic breakup of his family. In his mind, the only way to fix that problem so it did not happen again was to return to a very structured rule-based system. And religion worked well for him in that regard. Part of this process was breaking ties with much of his world. As a result, although I have tried numerous times to reconnect with Steve, we remain somewhat distant to this day.

For me, it was very different. I had come from a very strict religious view and moved into a more accepting form of spiritual philosophy. I grew to realize that the Source is the same, regardless of the religion or philosophical interpretation.

The challenge that impacts our unity is that we all seem to view the Source of spiritual growth a little differently. Like the proverbial story of the group of blind men describing an elephant, your perspective is different depending on where you touch the elephant. No one person is "right" and no one person is "wrong." In my friend Steve's case, it was difficult for me to understand how he could move so far back in the other direction. But when it comes down to it, I really don't need to understand. That is Steve's path and experience.

I accept now that people must find their own paths to understanding their individual life purposes. Our individual journeys are as unique as our fingerprints. As I look back on my time in Atlanta and at the chiropractic college, I am thankful for Steve and Mary and their willingness to share their philosophy, home, and hearts. They played a key role in my journey to move beyond my fear-mind by teaching me to let people have different perspectives without being judgmental. I was waking up to the other possibilities in life. I was beginning to leave fear and its wall-building judgment behind.

Meanwhile I had moved back home to Washington State and started to put my new degree to work. Beginning a new practice, paying bills, raising children, this didn't seem like what I had signed up for when I first started chiropractic school. And the church seemed less than enthusiastic about my life's mission.

I remember calling the treasurer of the North Pacific Union of Seventh-day Adventists requesting help in my moving expenses coming home from Atlanta. I had heard great stories of young doctors in my church receiving moving assistance and help starting their new practices. Instead, I was very abruptly told, "Sorry, we can only help medical doctors and dentists." In effect, I was hearing what Snoopy must have heard, "No dogs ALLOWWWED!" I recall being less than thrilled with the news and feeling quite indignant. What do you mean, "No chiropractors!"?

Then I remembered the reverence associated with medical doctors within the Adventist church. Adventist medicine had always been, and still is, in large part, a very traditional version of health care. Chiropractors were feared and probably accused of a long list of nefarious deeds. We were different and therefore suspect!

But how could I survive this life transition if no one would help me? Too penniless to qualify for a business loan, I remember starting my new office with about ten dollars in my pocket. Again hearing the same anti-chiropractic doctor sentiment from the loan officer at the local bank, my stubbornness and resolve only grew. Finding a suitable office suite, I negotiated with the building owner for just less than eight hundred square feet of space. It was an empty shell with no walls, sixteen feet wide and almost fifty feet deep. But it did have a restroom built in, lights in the ceiling, and heat. The owner gave me twelve hundred and fifty dollars to do the "build out" and I went to work. After hammering studs, nailing up sheetrock, mudding walls, and painting, in no time we had a very nice little office and we opened our doors.

The game had begun! Bring on the world! Let's get this healing stuff rockin'!

It was slow going. I remember one well-meaning person in the community—in fact I think she was my first "official" patient—telling me it would take about five years to get on my feet. Five years! But I've got to eat! My wife is pregnant with our firstborn! Five years?

And as you may have guessed, it took about five years to begin to pay the bills somewhat comfortably. One day early in our practice, one sweet lady, when she heard of our financial plight, sent us a card and said she had been "called" to help us. There was a check in the envelope for one thousand dollars. That was still quite a little bit of money to me in 1987. Her kind gesture was gratefully received!

I was still in survival mode, and little did I know my consciousness would remain fixed in that view of the universe for many long years. I didn't fully understand debt, its origin in fear, and the power it has in holding your life's progress seemingly absolutely still.

I was playing at life without fully understanding the rules. Blindly, I followed what I had been taught to believe was the only direction for my life to take. But greater understanding was on the horizon.

2

LEAVING THE TRIBE— IDENTIFYING FAMILY

"Love is the only force capable of transforming an enemy into friend."
— **Martin Luther King, Jr.**

You may look around at your family and wonder, "Who are these people and where did all of these nuts come from? Was I adopted or what?"

Thankfully, the universe is full of variety, and our families are no exception. While we may look alike physically, our personalities can be worlds apart! We all have certain buttons that our family members are experts at knowing how to push, so understanding how to manage the unique challenges our families present us is indeed an art.

Some people protect and guard themselves to the point of walking away from family. While I can understand the self-care this tactic represents, it can also mean the loss of a tremendous spiritual and emotional resource. Not to mention probably the best opportunity to learn about ourselves and our fear-minds.

I remember (actually my brother-in-law loves to remind me) of a Christmas holiday years ago that some of us in the family affectionately refer to as the "Christmas in Hell." My wife and I had decided "Wouldn't it be great if we could get both sides of the family together this Christmas?" While our hearts were in the right place, unfortunately, our brains were somewhere on the dark side of Mars.

So we innocently arranged to rent a couple of vacation houses on the Oregon coast for a week, and blissfully, and of course ignorantly, proceeded with the orchestration of the fateful event.

Picture a few dozen loosely associated relatives, many tender egos, and several emotionally challenged folks under one roof, many miles from home (for all of us). The holiday started out innocently enough; in fact, the first few hours were actually quite pleasant. Then things started to unravel. Pets showed up. Smokers were offended by the rules. Comments from various factions were made on the numbers of gifts, an obvious disparity evident in how Christmas traditions were cherished in the differing households. Tongues wagged, sparks flew, and doors slammed. Some say the scars are still visible, the fires still smoldering.

This experience showed me that apparently some things are destined to be learned the hard way. And arguably, the challenging lessons are the most valuable. Possibly even the most painful. But who's to say? In the end, I think I have to agree with Eckhart Tolle: Pain is there to bring us back into the classroom. My friend, Bob Trask, has always reminded me, "Pain is inevitable in life, while suffering is optional."

As we bring lessons into our lives, pain will surface in direct proportion to our resistance (or the fear-mind's involvement). How long the pain continues depends on our level of resistance to and awareness or consciousness in the process. If we allow ourselves to attract using our fear-mind, the result will be a life lesson appropriate to the amount of fear. The more conscious we are, the less dramatic the lesson. So the good news is, the longer we "stay in school," the less likely the suffering. The "bad" news is that each time we learn a valuable life lesson, we invite the next, more challenging lesson into our lives. And likely more pain.

Regarding family challenges, bottom line, my recommendation is, even though your heart is in the right place, tread wisely when considering large family reunions—especially when invitations are made across married family lines. Don't be pushy when it comes to tender egos and sensitive fear-minds. Allow the process to unfold for others in their own time, in their own way.

If you can invite people together who are willing to stretch and learn, who are aware of their fear-minds, these events can be stepping-stones to huge strides in personal spiritual growth. On the other hand, if the challenge and opportunity for growth is resisted, you can at least enjoy the fireworks and drama!

The wild card is that we are all at different mileposts in our journeys through life. Expectations of meeting at the same rest area with common goals and outlooks are unrealistic at the very least. Give yourself a break. Step back, love, and observe. Stop trying to fix the others in your family. You have a big enough job with the individual in your bathroom mirror.

"Personal relationships are the fertile soil from which all advancement, all success, all achievement in real life grows."
— Ben Stein

How do we love and respect our families, yet still retain the integrity of a spiritual environment?

The Bible says to "Honor thy father and mother that thy days may be long." Do seniority and familial ties guarantee respect? Can age give wisdom and therefore command that respect? Not always!

A quote in Richard Bach's book *Illusions* actually shocked me many years ago: "*The people that live under the same roof as you, are not necessarily your family.*" What if your "family," the people who unconditionally support you in your path, are not the ones who share your name and/or blood? How bound are you by the biblical directive of "Honor thy father and mother"? If those who share your DNA are dragging you into a spiritual sewer, what is your responsibility to yourself?

Good questions. No easy answers. The simple answer would be to go out and create a family that supports. Oh, but then there is GUILT! Who would I be if I walked away from my family? And does the self-care of removing myself from negative influences mean I am not respecting my family?

I choose to believe that our first responsibility is to our Divine self. Some would say to God. In that I am in agreement and the difference is only one of semantics. We are first responsible to our spiritual wholeness and wellness. Only then can we relate with integrity to our family. So to suffer emotional and spiritual abuse, just because the contaminating influence is "family," is not the best answer in my opinion.

This lesson has been a tough one for me, and I know it is for others as well. None of us initially feels good about separating ties, even unhealthy ones. But the results can be healing. AND you will likely find that those who participate in unhealthy relationships will, by your initiative, find healing in their lives as well. The important factor is to remember that first you must take care of yourself.

I rarely listen to the instructions given by flight attendants when getting ready to take off on a commercial airline flight. But what always grabs my attention is the instruction first to place the oxygen on your own face, and then attend to those near you who need assistance.

Makes lots of sense doesn't it? It is no different in your spiritual path. An impaired person is of no assistance to others. Our spiritual health is no exception. See to yourself. Be very selfish. This paradoxically is the path to a fulfilling life of service. Do not let your fear-mind tell you otherwise!

Believe me, the world will try to convince you that almost any self-care is selfish. Observe the argument, nod politely, and then move on to your primary purpose. You will be able to be of service to thousands more if you are spiritually, emotionally, and physically strong. There is no other way. To be convinced otherwise is fallacy.

"You can observe a lot just by watching."
— Yogi Berra

When we are concerned about the welfare of our family, it is helpful to remember we are ALL on separate and unique spiritual paths. To expect your personal agenda to be followed by another is to judge and not allow.

I first met my friend Steve S. when he was working for UPS. He delivered our packages and even eventually became a chiropractic patient. Over the years, we got to know each other better out in the great outdoors.

Steve took me to new heights, literally. We climbed to the summit of Mt. Rainier twice together, Mt. Hood once, and just missed planting the flag on Washington's Mt. Baker due to truly nasty weather.

One of the scariest experiences of my life was in the summer of 1995 on the western slopes of Mt. Rainier. It was definitely the most intense storm I have experienced in my life, and it did its best to sweep us off the glacier above St. Andrews Park. We had intended to summit this more difficult route, and we spent over two days just reaching the glacier's upper approaches. We found a beautiful, gently sloped bowl behind the ridge to camp for the night, eager to break camp in the morning and tackle the summit route. During the night, hurricane force winds picked up, compelling us to spend a very long night struggling to keep the tents from being ripped off the mountain. After waking up to a foot and a half of fresh snow and one of the most beautiful sights I have ever witnessed, we wisely decided to turn around and try another day.

I am forever indebted to Steve's wisdom for this decision to turn back. A man less wise would have probably pushed through, risking lives for the benefit of ego. Steve, thankfully, and true to his nature, resisted the strong urge to "get there" and put everyone in danger. He knew the mountains. He allowed them to be without inserting his idea of what was best.

My fear-mind and its pushing sure can get me into trouble. Usually, it is as mild as an inadvertent foot in the mouth; however, at times it has put my life in danger. Fear pushes; it does not allow. Allow your family members to climb the mountain of discovery at their own paces. Your family life will be much more peaceful.

Quiet observation and allowing is true power. Forced, fear-based action or "re-activity" is unproductive and even extremely dangerous.

Today, I have learned to have my experiences and let others have theirs without trying to control or change them, and without offering advice unless they come to me looking for it. In the past, I have been very unforgiving of what I don't understand, and with my family members, I have been impatient while trying to figure out why they act the way they do. Now I have learned that to criticize, judge, or point out others' errors is not only insensitive—it also does not fix the problem. This change in me has allowed me to maintain both family ties and my sanity.

I highly recommend the practiced art of allowing in the area of family relationships. With a little love and acknowledgment, your family can be among your biggest fans and offer you unparalleled support as you grow, experience, and learn in this life.

3
SURVIVING THE PAIN OF SEPARATION:
I LEAVE MY CHURCH FAMILY

"Religion exists to block a direct experience of God."
— Carl Jung

When I first read this quote by Jung, I was deeply offended. Obviously, this "God-less" man was very far from any understanding of religion. I was again judgmental of what I did not understand. Religion is spirituality, isn't it? Isn't that how we humans approach and find out about God?

At that time, I was still in denial about how I had allowed organized religion to create for me a life of fear. Fear excludes inspiration and eventually your spiritual connection to Source. When you are identified with fear and lack, you are estranged from this spiritual source, and the result will be that your energy, your attractive resonance will only invite in more lack and fear.

In my years of chiropractic practice, I have become better at identifying people locked in the survival existence of fear. A common manifestation of this fear is some form of physical malady, and my recognition is less from the list of symptoms on the intake form, and more from the person's facial expression and the slow transformation toward illness visible in the body.

A common segment of the population that exhibits these symptoms, at least among my patients, is in the thirty to fifty-year old range. The majority tend to be female. These women often seek chiropractic care with a tremendous list of physical ailments, including chronic fatigue, fibromyalgia, or some other example of a vague physical disorder.

At first I was puzzled, but then I began to see a pattern, and having been a Seventh-day Adventist helped me put two and two together. The fear-based belief system of the conservative Christian, in this case Adventist Christian, often seemed to create a physical manifestation of headaches, back and neck pain, and depression. I got to the point where I could recognize the cause of pain before I knew the patient's background. Many patients' physical symptoms were the result of frantically trying to conform to a code of belief and conduct that was at the same time destroying their physical and spiritual energy.

These women were being taught by religious doctrine that they were inherently faulty. And their belief that they were flawed was manifesting itself physically. Even if it would have been appropriate to do so, no amount of arguing otherwise would have been sufficient to convince them of their worthiness. They seemed to be caught in a whirlpool of despair without hope of escape. The result was physical and mental deterioration.

Prescription drug use is typically rampant in this group, which almost always only adds to more physical side-effects. Some of these patients finally succumbed to the last resort, leaving traditional medicine and consulting a chiropractor. This decision in itself was remarkable, since the Adventist Church historically has viewed chiropractors as beneath any level of professional respectability. In fact, we have for many years been labeled as quacks and at the very least, unscientific. Okay, I am being a bit dramatic here, but not by much.

Several years ago, when I was younger, more foolish, and filled with an irrepressible evangelical zeal for chiropractic, I became aware of the crusade against chiropractic led by Dr. William Jarvis.

Jarvis, founder of the National Council Against Health Fraud, made a name for himself by taking up what he considered a worthy cause and his sacred duty—to rid the planet of the heretical scourge called chiropractic. His council determined the chiropractic profession was fraudulent and dangerous to the general public's health. Of course, this belief is without merit and the U.S. justice system has since declared chiropractic is neither fraudulent nor dangerous.

When I found out Dr. Jarvis was a fellow Adventist, I was shocked, embarrassed, and a bit ashamed. At the time, I was still a member of the Adventist church and engaged in my own futile attempts to convince the church of my chosen profession's value.

After discovering Jarvis was a professor of public health at Loma Linda University, a prominent Adventist institution, I decided to contact him with hopes of beginning a healthy discussion as to the merits of each of our professions. My naïve hope was that with understanding, we could agree to disagree and allow each other the freedom to live, practice, and share the oxygen on this planet without the need to destroy each other.

When I made the call, I was surprised that the receptionist let me talk to him right away. After I introduced myself, I briefly explained my purpose for calling. When I finished speaking, the line went silent. It was a bit like a scene from a horror movie. It can only be described as pure malevolence somehow being transferred inaudibly over the telephone connection. I will never forget how that felt. Needless to say, the conversation was very brief and very unproductive. There was no hope for continuing dialogue. He had no interest in speaking further to the likes of me.

This taught me a lot about the fear-mind. We humans tend to destroy what we do not understand. The agenda of the National Council Against Health Fraud was to discredit and destroy the largest non-drug, non-surgical health system on the planet. Period.

This experience went a long way toward convincing me that perhaps I was attending and contributing to the wrong church. I found this conclusion difficult to accept when my whole life, most of my family, friends, and support structure happened to warm the pews of this endearing institution each Sabbath. But I was starting to question what I was beginning to see as narrow-minded views and an unwillingness to consider any other possibilities beyond what the Seventh-day Adventist Church believed.

Of course, it is not just one church. All religions require adherence and obedience in order to maintain the allegiance of their members. Free-thinking is okay to a small degree, but if you start to question the church's core beliefs, its members tend to get very uncomfortable. When belief systems get stepped on and questioned, even long-held friendships are endangered. Is your blood pressure or indignation rising as you read these words? If so, can you understand why?

My understanding is that life is meant to be lived in joy, exploration, and wonder. My experience with religion is that it tends to edge out joy with the harsh application of rules, belief systems, and standards. The argument I usually hear is that without these standards, chaos, anarchy, murder, and mayhem ensue. In my experience, this argument has proven to be an exaggeration to say the least.

Church attendance does not guarantee a person is filled with the values of acceptance, love, and support. In fact, many times it has the opposite effect. How truly pleasant and accepting can a person be who is constantly concerned with whether his conduct is right or wrong?

If we are born in fear, nurtured in fear, and controlled in the environment of fear, can we really expect to experience joy as a result?

In my experience, religion can only teach you what will support the organization and its accepted belief system. I absorbed the message to be a "good boy" like a sponge and latched my reason for existing to perfecting the art of knowing right versus wrong. My striving to "be" good was constantly reinforced by the church as were the mixed messages in the teaching that we are born incomplete. One hand was holding out the carrot of intense bliss, while the other hand was pointing to the shame and incompleteness of being born estranged from God.

From my earliest days in my church, I was told the Bible was God's divinely inspired gift to us. It was our guidance system to "Heaven." What I wasn't told was that the Bible was incomplete. Like a letter from Russia during the Cold War, not only words, but entire books and chapters were cut out! Entire gospels were deleted simply because their messages conflicted with the beliefs of those in the early church who had placed themselves in a position to decide what should be "inspired" and what content labeled spurious.

The First Council of Nicaea, held in 325 A.D., edited the content of what we now know as the "complete" Bible. Like a government censor with sharp scissors, the Council snipped out a gospel here, a gospel there. The result was a finished product of exceptional and glorious deception.

My early church-based instruction, even though clothed in beautiful music and rhetoric, was one founded on the language of fear. "Whoever adds to or deletes from the book" was in danger of eternal separation from God, from Source. This was not a command to be taken lightly. You did not question the validity of the Book.

Ironically, the ones proclaiming this dire judgment were the very ones holding the scissors!

I know with my own children that when I forbid them to watch, read, or do something, it makes what is forbidden irresistible. This is the mystique of forbidden fruit!

Over the years, I noticed a slow, insidious exodus of young people from my local church. This pattern was mirrored in many other Adventist churches as well. At first, the blame was attributed to the lure of the outside world, which was drawing them away from the purity of the church. Sin is attractive, I was told. But I continued to work hard at doing the right thing. I felt great pride in being the one who stayed with the church. My schedule soon filled to overflowing with choir practices, church board meetings, school board meetings, and church youth group gatherings. All good stuff. But something was missing.

Life appeared to be good, but a vague uneasiness was mounting in me. Any tendency to stray was kept at bay by the rewards of church membership. I loved the singing, the potlucks, and the fellowship. As a "people-person," I fit into the social crowd, my sense of service largely fulfilled by church-provided programs.

Yet a piece of my life was missing. Something was wrong. My level of awareness at that time was so low that I saw no intellectual, tangible answer for my unease. I don't even think I was aware at the time that anything was really "wrong." At the time, I mistook religion for spirituality. What I thought was

God and Spirit had ironically been distorted by the church and more importantly, by me.

But eventually, I couldn't help but attract an event to initiate my next chapter in life. So I co-created my divorce and the resulting separation from my church. Painful though the process was, the resultant change in environment and direction opened for me a window of consciousness. I was able to find myself spiritually. Over a long period, my life responded with growth, searching, and listening. A sense of who I really was began to fill me.

My relationship with my church ended coincidentally with my divorce. Actually the events were a bit intertwined.

The Pastor

After seventeen years of marriage, my divorce was a very traumatic experience. I had invested most of my life and a tremendous amount of energy into building the image of spirituality in my life.

The year prior to my divorce, I was president of my high school alumni association. I was also president of the local Rotary club, involved in the local church school board, and held an elder's position in the church. I was the very picture of the contributing, involved family man. But inside I had reached the wall. I couldn't do it any longer. I could no longer pretend to be what I wasn't while searching for what I couldn't explain.

Pastor Ron and his wife came to the church a year or so before my marriage began to unravel. As luck would have it (not mine of course) the pastor's wife was a family friend of my wife's family in Idaho. When I think of this lady, the old "Saturday Night Live" skits of the "Church Lady" come to mind. Since I really try not to speak negatively of others, it's sufficient to say her righteousness was without equal in our church.

Once my first wife and I separated and it became well known in the church and community that our divorce was imminent, I received a phone call from the pastor. I remember clearly the relief I felt that at long last, someone was reaching out to me! The whispers were starting to wear on me. As a professional in the community with many of my patients coming from the local congregation, the rumors of my marital problems were starting to affect my practice as well. Having always loved the association of my church friends and acquaintances and also having always enjoyed the social aspect of the church, the more recent coolness bordering on shunning was starting to have a very negative impact on my life.

I recall arriving at the church with great expectation and being ushered into the inner sanctum of the pastor's office. Walking into the pastor's study, I was a bit surprised to see the pastor's wife standing next to him, but I assumed she was present as well to offer her support and help me through this very trying time.

Boy was I in for a surprise! Nowhere on either face could I detect a trace of friendship, sympathy, or anything close to a desire to help. I had somehow unwittingly stumbled into some sort of hastily contrived tribunal!

After a few mumbled half-hearted niceties, the tone of conversation quickly turned to my pitiful circumstance and the error of my ways. I was summarily informed that if I did not turn from my wicked course of action, terrible things would befall me. And not just me!

The good pastor proceeded to inform me that if I did not immediately turn from my evil path, each of my four sons would grow up to be an adulterer, a ne'er-do-well, even a murderer! At first I could not believe what I was hearing. I looked into their eyes and was met with rigid silence. My shock must have been comical to behold! I remember the overbearing, malevolent presence and look from the churchly matriarch. Although I don't remember her saying much, her stare was penetrating, and I could sense that Pastor Ron was like a puppet on a stick. By the uncomfortable way he looked and moved, I am pretty sure I know where that stick was inserted!

My departure from the church that day was both hasty and very numbing. As I got back into my car, I looked at the bricks of the beautiful building, many of which my own hands had laid. I remembered the many years, the joy, the happiness, and the friends. And now this. It was devastating to me.

It wasn't long before the church was urged to take action and expel me from its membership. A church general membership meeting was called, I believe after a Sabbath evening potluck, and a vote was taken that removed me from membership for "apostasy." I heard later that a certain measure of resistance and solidarity occurred from among the cooler heads in attendance, and many of my friends stood up for me, but the church had to be cleansed. And so it was.

Today my wife Melanie likes to refer to this event as my "dis-memberment" or to say that I was "dis-membered." And that is exactly how it felt—like part of me had been traumatically ripped away. Today I can more easily understand that, based on what I know the congregation's level of consciousness and fear was at the time, the church members sincerely believed they were doing the right thing. But to me it just felt bad.

With the passage of time, I am now so thankful for the action taken that day. As bad as it felt then, those events helped propel me into the uncertain world of discovery, accountability, and spiritual reason. They helped me see the extent of our fear-based belief systems and what adherence to these beliefs can drive people to do to one another. I am in no way diminishing my accountability and participation in this event; however, I am now very aware of what religion is capable of and what it can lead people to do in "God's" name.

My Uncle Marvin in California, a very respected man with decades of service in the church, was appalled at what had transpired. True, his concern was undoubtedly a trifle biased. His ensuing inquiries and indignation at the events eventually led to the removal of this pastor from the Adventist ministry. I understand that today this man exercises a very minor administrative position somewhere within the bowels of the church, probably the lower end. In truth, this gives me no satisfaction; to be honest, the feelings brought forth are more akin to empathy than anything. I can still clearly see his face and level of discomfort from that day so long ago.

In retrospect, I think on some level I secretly wanted my church "dis-memberment" to occur, and therefore, consciously acted as a co-creator of the situation.

I am now convinced that a person will create (or co-create) any circumstance in his life that will assist him in learning the life lessons at the top of his cosmic syllabi. And there seems to be a direct relationship between the severity and importance of each lesson. There appear to be no shortcuts. A lesson avoided is just cycled back into our list for an even more potent opportunity for growth later on.

So in the end, I am grateful for my church giving me the boot.

As Carl Jung stated, religion can prevent a direct experience of God, and I agree. Religions typically are enforced belief systems—systems with inherent fear-mind flaws that motivate men to actions based in fear, and therefore, are likely to produce a suppression of spiritual growth.

I have discovered that religion is not necessarily synonymous with an understanding of Spirit, who our Creator is, and who we are. At best, it can be a poor reflection of Spirit expression IF the fear-based ego can be kept at bay. True spiritual growth seems to occur in spite of religion rather than as a result of it. Of this I am convinced.

"You do not have to struggle to reach God, but you do have to struggle to tear away the self-created veil that hides him from you."
— **Paramahansa Yogananda**

I truly hold no anger toward my church today. Only sympathy, empathy, and sometimes sorrow. My sons have had the benefit of witnessing each of their parents' experiences. Their life journey today is a testament to the value of that multifaceted education. Not that it was easy by any stretch of the imagination; however, I believe they have developed a healthy, open-eyed awareness of religion and a deep understanding of how best to discover their own innate spirituality. Of this I am so grateful. Everything has been worth it. I have no regrets.

My counsel to all those who read these words is to take a careful, objective look at your belief systems, especially those relating to your tribal beliefs or those associated with any ecclesiastical membership. In my opinion, this is vital for spiritual health. For a person to observe accurately where he or she is on a spiritual path, one needs to see it objectively, without the unclear, false interpretation of the fear-mind.

This objective look is not easy to accomplish. Most of us have a tremendous amount of emotional attachment to our church families. To obtain an objective high ground from which to observe any barriers to our spiritual growth, some separation must occur. And to break the hold of the fear-mind frequently requires a shock or trauma in our lives. That is how strong our belief systems are!

Our fear-mind fears for its very existence when deeply held belief systems are challenged! The intensity of defense is proportionate with the intensity of the threat. Our identity is fighting for its life! It is no wonder wars are fought and millions of people have died in the name of "God" and in the defense of what is "right." This is necessary only if suffering is needed to break the hold of the fear-mind identification.

With awareness arrives the opportunity to make a change in conscious identity without the accompanying trauma. Suffering does not have to be! We can allow and nurture our spiritual growth rather than permitting our fear-minds to continue attacking what they do not and cannot understand. With awareness comes the gift of choice. And in that order. Without this awareness, we will continue to create pain and uncomfortable opportunities for spiritual growth.

"The great majority of choices made by human beings are not properly so called at all, but are mere acquiescence in a compulsive desire from the unconscious."
— **Helen M. Luke**

I absolutely love seeing that beautiful glimmer of knowing that lights up the eyes of those who choose to see! Especially when I glimpse that light in my own eye when I bring a mirror into my life! And I sure attract mirrors! I have learned that each teacher in my life is my mirror. Each one is another opportunity to understand and quiet my fear-mind. For each precious one I am eventually grateful, although in truth, the initial flavor can be quite unpleasant. But I learn, and I grow. That is my path on this earth, in this expression of Spirit. Again, I give thanks.

Please don't drive away your teachers—those beautiful souls that your fear-mind labels as enemies. Some day you will understand you were the one who invited them. You will undertake the accountability of knowing that each "crisis" in your life is of your own making. You will come to know that each one is a gift, and each time you refuse the gift, it will return, again by your invitation, with greater intensity. Of this I am certain.

Learn to extend graciously the hand of a loving host to each mirror you invite into your life. This is the measure of spiritual growth. It may take your entire lifetime (or maybe many more) to come to this knowing. And that is okay. No one is keeping score. You are not being judged. There is no "short bus" in the universal highway system. We are all on our paths based on the all-knowing design team, of which we are members.

It kind of takes the pressure off, doesn't it? To remove both the outer and inner judge lends a sense of love and allowing that cannot be present in the fear paradigm.

It is helpful to dedicate the first few moments of each day to reminding yourself of who YOU are and the capability of your fear-mind to entice you to re-identify with fear and pain. It will tell you that because the world is a dangerous place, you have to fight for everything worth having. Your identification with fear will do its best to feed the ego's insatiable desire for drama, fear, pain, and suffering.

You can learn to break the cycle with the simple exercise of quiet observation. Light dissolves darkness into itself. Darkness doesn't exist! It is merely the absence of light! Your power of observation sheds light on the illusory power of the darkness. All it takes is a simple reminder of what is real and what is not.

As this discipline of observing becomes more natural for you, you will begin attracting people and circumstances into your life to support your life's work. Your fear-mind will likely interpret these lessons as "problems" and do its best to create drama and reactivity in order to feed its need for pain and disorder.

If you view these opportunities as gifts to yourself, you can choose to see each day as a kind of Christmas morning, a chance to unwrap an exciting new gift!

"Once you believe that answers and resources can show up in your life, they will: The universe works to mirror your beliefs. It will prove you right every time."
— **Peggy McColl**

When we allow the perpetuation of the fear-mind view, each opportunity for growth in understanding is instead viewed as a problem and a threat. If we overcome the threat with a fear-motivated response, the ego views it as a win, and even if we appear to be defeated, we assume the identity of the victim, which is again a win for the fear-motivated ego.

Remember that our fear identity has only the measure of power we give it. By observing the fear, we remove its power and return the ego to the status of a servant, where the ego belongs. This is both empowering in a healthy way and an incredible confidence-builder from which to lay a foundation for joyful living. In the chapters that follow, I'll share more about how I started on my journey of observing fear and learning to keep it in its place.

4

SEEKING SALVATION

*"Sometimes your joy is the source of your smile,
but sometimes your smile can be the source
of your joy."*
— Thich Nhat Hanh

Why am I Here? Where did I come From? Where am I going? What is my purpose here?

So many questions! And so many difficult answers! I had allowed myself to believe that my church had the answers thoughtfully contained in the incredible leather-bound Book. As my life experiences progressed, I soon found that the safety of those answers was becoming increasingly suspect.

I was told, and soon believed, that if you kept the Sabbath, tithed faithfully, studied the Sabbath school lesson, and participated in church functions, you could be assured of spiritual and physical security. At least eventually. Heaven was the goal and reward for those who lived by the Book and whose names were written in THE Book. From as early as I can remember, I did my best to be the good boy. I avoided drinking, dancing, going to movies (for the most part), and many other activities deemed by the church as "sinful" or at least distracting to our real purpose. While a few of my friends enjoyed some rather delicious detours into the worldly life, I kept my slate clean, attended church, participated in "worthy" activities, and hoped and prayed it was all good enough.

"You find God when you realize that you don't need to seek God."
— Eckhart Tolle

Then life happened. Divorce, church dis-fellowship, avoidance, and even shunning by former friends. I was amazed at how the safe, warm world could turn so cold so quickly. Lifelong friends suddenly and without asking for my version of the drama, did their duty by casting their ballots for my exclusion. As painful as the process was, I was also amazed! This was actually happening to me!

In truth, it took many years to get past the feelings of being wronged and a victim of such an unjust process. Now in retrospect, I am so very thankful for the opportunity to explore the world outside of the Adventist church! A world I had previously held in such great fear and distrust I now found populated by people who could be kind, supportive, and even lovable!

As time went by, the pain and sense of loss was gradually replaced with the wonder of discovery. What I had previously understood as spirituality, I now quickly realized was religious dogma cleverly masquerading as spirituality, and these belief systems were sadly inadequate in dealing with larger life questions and challenges.

True salvation, I learned, is really freedom from fear, freedom from the tyranny of the fear-mind. Salvation is not "some day" or "somewhere," in a "heaven" in a galaxy far, far away in some distant dimension. True spiritual salvation is now and only obscured from us by the fear-mind and its manifestation.

About a year after my separation from my (first) wife and then the church, I became a client of a consulting firm for chiropractic practices taught by a doctor in southern California. While moderately successful in building my practice over the years, I was looking for a way to become more successful and reach out to more people. At first, as I moved further away from the safe confines of the church, my exposure to more expanded forms of understanding was quite frightening. But in these seminars, surrounded by my chiropractic friends, I felt safe to explore such experiences as fire walking and bending construction re-bar (by walking toward another person with the bar against one's throat). These and other experiences challenged deeply my long-held B.S. (belief systems), but while they were frightening, my mind was open to the possibilities they held. As time went on, I experienced a degree of heightened understanding and awareness; however, the goal to find "the answer" still seemed to evade me.

My personal and professional coaches attributed my slow spiritual growth to being too "stuck in my head." But the harder I tried to think my way out of the "stuck in the head" problem, the more elusive was the release from its spiritually numbing grip. My frustration increased.

After a series of seminars, experiential retreats, and a few rather expensive years of coaching, I was really getting discouraged. Why did this have to be so difficult? It didn't appear to me that anyone else was having anything close to this degree of difficulty. Apparently I believed I was "special."

Then about six or seven years ago, I was invited to attend an office building/team building retreat for chiropractic professionals in the north cascades of Washington State. Dave, a fellow chiropractor and good friend, highly recommended I come and "check it out." I was eager to set the stage for a fun and exciting new year in the office, so I committed myself and my office team to the retreat.

My new wife Melanie and I spent a wonderful weekend in the north Cascade Mountains at a beautiful lodge in the Methow Valley along with fifty or so other people, many of them chiropractors and staff who had come together to plan and set goals for the coming year.

At the retreat, I met a self-empowerment trainer and life coach by the name of Bob Trask. Bob had been teaching, training, and coaching since the "good ole' days" of the 1970s EST trainings—the hardcore "sink or swim" model of personal transformation and enlightenment.

I still remember clearly the impact of my first encounter with Bob and his teaching philosophy. His quiet, purposeful intensity was a refreshing departure from my earlier experiences with my church, practice, and previous life coaches. His assured, confident manner quickly set aside my fear of again wasting my time and money looking for "the answer."

Bob spoke that day about Spirit and accountability. By accountability, he meant moving through life with purpose, prepared for and anticipating change and the challenges that come with taking a close look at long held belief systems. Bob introduced me to the concept of the workings of the ego, the fear-based mind, and how we defend our "swamp," that collection of experiences and belief systems that tend to mold and shape our day-to-day experience.

I was introduced to a completely new way of thinking about life and purpose. At least it was new for me since my wife had embraced these concepts many years earlier (and was patiently waiting for me to wake up!). I discovered I was not a victim of circumstance, but rather, I could actually discover a purpose in life other than a futile grasping at some far-off utopia. I learned I could appreciate and learn from my past without letting my past dictate my present identity. I also learned my future need to arrive (for example, to have a future goal such as to reach Heaven) could be replaced with an appreciation of the present.

This was a true eye-opener for me. I realized I had "wasted" so many years of my life in a hasty stampede toward an ethereal goal. Like a mirage continually disappearing as I drew near, the illusion of salvation and gratification in the future had always evaporated. Instead, I realized that "Life is right now!"

By the time the retreat concluded, I was sure I was onto something deeply significant and purposeful in my life. My wife and I would work with Bob over the next three to four years in a combination of personal coaching/counseling and a series of seminars that totally changed my understanding and paradigm of who I was and what my purpose in life was or could be. My victim identity was dying!

However, it was not to be a quiet, graceful death. The fear-mind (ego) equates this sort of identity shift with actual death. I was to find that the ensuing defensiveness of ego over the next three or four years was both exhilarating and at times excruciating. In retrospect, it is amazing to me that my wife Melanie and I were able to move together through the experience without tearing each other apart! I can only describe it as an unspoken, subconscious knowing that the process would deliver an understanding and growth that at the time would not have been understood. There is a lot to be said for naïve ignorance in the face of change!

Melanie and I soon decided to see Bob for some regular spiritual and relationship counseling. We had recently married— the second marriage for both of us—so we looked forward to his gentle, encouraging method of helping to take a close look at how we navigated life.

Several subsequent retreats on the Hawaiian island of Molokai gave us the opportunity to learn more about Bob's unique way of looking at the human experience. Over the years Bob developed a version of the "be-do-have" cycle that had become a common tool in empowerment training workshops. The "Trask Triangle" graphically portrays our journey through change and awareness.

We begin at rest. As we contemplate change, we put together our support team and move toward the risky part: Change. It's well-known that many people would rather die than change, but this thought really comes from the fear-mind, the ego that is "scared to death" of change. As we move around "the top" of the triangle, and move toward the "win" or the "have," we acknowledge our worthiness; we realize we have successfully gained ground spiritually instead of choosing the alternative: avoidance and despair.

Then we have the opportunity to celebrate the win with rest, rejuvenation, and joy. We are again able to set our sight on a new vision, confidently moving through a new experience and acquiring yet another new and invigorating identity.

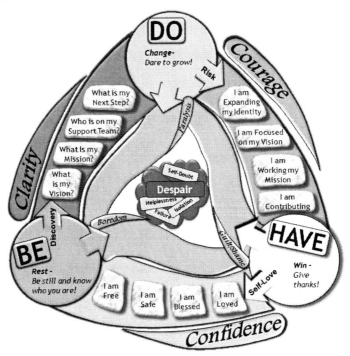

Vision quests on Molokai also introduced me to the Native American tradition of connection to creation or Great Spirit. Our western belief system has taken on the identity of the fear-mind and its conviction that we are separate and distant from Source. As I experienced my newfound knowledge and understanding of my personal connection with Spirit, I realized how weak and fragile the religious world was for me. Rules and doctrine were taking me further away from my Creator. A gulf was being created by the very means I had assumed were connecting me with God.

When I discovered how religion had separated me from God, I first felt betrayed. But mixed with this sense of betrayal was the emotional trauma of leaving behind all I had known and held dear. Safety was in the church. I had learned well that anything "spiritual" outside the walls of the Adventist church was falsehood. I had been stuck between the proverbial "rock and a hard place." No wonder there was so much physical and emotional illness in the church!

It was then that I began to see that God was not "out there." He was here. Within me. I was a beautiful manifestation of Spirit. I was worthy beyond measure. Just as I experienced my unconditional love for my children, God's love was without condition. No amount of adherence to rules could enhance my position in the "kingdom."

It took time, many years, to get over the innate need to "do something" to be okay spiritually. I still struggle with this concept, so deeply is this need for effort ingrained in my core beliefs. The "peace that passes understanding" is the knowing that I am connected to my Source, that God is right here, right now.

My relationship with Bob, due largely to his Native American upbringing and traditions, had introduced me to new experiences and an opportunity for having my belief systems severely challenged. These are lessons I have retained and applied in my own opportunities to mentor and teach. I feel forever blessed and thankful for his friendship, mentoring, and instruction.

Along with what I learned from Bob, another key moment in my spiritual awakening was my introduction to Chester, whom, surprisingly, I had known all along, but that's a story deserving its own section!

SECTION
2

THE VOICE

5

DISCOVERING CHESTER

"A crack in the wall."

My mother insists I was born with a smile on my face. I began life happy, laughing and truly enjoying everything around me. She tells me of how as a baby, when put down for a nap, I would playfully stick my head up and grin. She would lovingly tell me to put my head down and go to sleep. Then my head would pop up again and with a twinkle in my eye, I would wait for another reminder to go to sleep. It became a game I loved to play.

Then somewhere along the way, life became a serious game. I increasingly lost the ability to laugh. I grew up. Life not only developed into a contest that delivered immediate consequences, but one with life and death spiritual ramifications as well. I learned my worthiness depended greatly on which day of the week I worshipped. Having too much fun on the Sabbath was severely frowned upon by many. One of my favorite jokes today is, "Why don't Adventists have sex standing up?" Answer: "Because it might lead to dancing!" The joke wasn't so funny back when I first heard it, but today, it is not only very funny but incredibly insightful.

I recall Saturday (Sabbath) mornings before going to church as very painful experiences, my mother in tears, and my father looking as if he preferred to be on another continent. They, like me, were raised with a strict code of what was "right" and what was "wrong." It was "right" to make sure the family went to church in respectable clothes each Saturday morning, never mind that they were both exhausted after a long week of work. Church was where everyone put on a smiling face for Jesus and where everyone did his or her best to "be" the kind of Adventist the church found worthy. This pressure, and a multitude of other worries and fears I can only guess at, contributed to the angst of Sabbath morning preparations.

We kids were just trying to navigate through the day without making a big mistake or getting in serious trouble. And all of this was in preparation for attending church with the purpose of serving a loving God, and of course, with hopes of cashing in on the ultimate lottery win of a lifetime: everlasting life in Heaven with Jesus.

This way of living was a bit stressful to say the least, but of course, it was not always a grim picture. Yes, we had happy times, but always an undercurrent of tension was in the background.

A striving to "be good," with constant reinforcement by the church that we were born incomplete, unworthy, and "in sin," and then the mixed messages of Grace and Original Sin were a lot to wrap my young mind around.

Looking back, it seems incredible! Who could have possibly created a better way to mess with a young person's mind? With one hand, the church was holding out a carrot of eternal happiness and bliss, while with the other hand, it was pointing out the shame and unworthiness of being born disconnected from God.

I recently saw a very insightful movie by the comedian Bill Maher called *Religulous*. It's a very entertaining and irreverent attempt to point out the incredible silliness of religion and its attempts to explain spirituality. Bravo to Bill! Although, I am sure he is now on most churches' "do not play" lists. I did enjoy the film, but I cannot imagine I would have been receptive to it at all when I was deep within the church.

I have learned that the only way to see the spiritual shortcomings of religion is with a bit of distance, a luxury not typically found by the "religious" sort. This perspective usually must be found through separation trauma of some sort. When you are within the "fold," you are spiritually secure to the point of not feeling the need of any help, particularly in the spiritual sense. All you need the church will give you. Don't worry about it and be careful about asking too many questions!

The space I needed to obtain a measure of objectivity in regard to my spiritual health was created by intense emotional trauma, an event I perceived at the time from a "victim" point of view, even though at some level, it was more than likely subconsciously desired. At least that is how I see it in retrospect. I "knew" for years that "something" was missing in my life; yet at that time, I thought it was something external. I remember an intense longing I tried to fill with church, duty, and work, but the longing continued and grew nevertheless.

Then came a crack in the wall. I was somehow able to create a way out and through my dilemma, unconscious though the action was. The incident occurred that would initiate my eventual separation from the church.

A year or so before my divorce was final and after having separated from my wife of seventeen years, I had the privilege of attending a Promise Keepers convention at the Kingdome in Seattle. At that time, I had very recently moved back in with my wife and we were attempting to reconcile. I was to attend the convention with a small group of guys who met weekly at a local prayer breakfast. I remember being less than eager to go, probably because I felt like the token Adventist going to an event primarily attended by Sunday observers. At any rate, I went. I remember sitting in the Dome and looking around at another 70,000 or so very motivated Christian men. This was not a quiet event! What I do remember with most impact was the music! Impressive!

Seventy thousand male voices raised in boisterous praise is quite an experience. It struck a chord in me that has vibrated ever since. As the music built, I felt something give, what I can only explain now as a "crack" in the wall around my heart. Tears flowed. That experience will never leave me. The effect and change was life altering.

When I returned home, life was different. I'm not saying the wounds were gone and life was "peachy." No, actually everything pretty much went to hell. My wife and I ended up not reconciling and my life entered a new phase.

With this epiphany, a period of intense restlessness began. The songs and activities at church just didn't do it for me anymore. I was dissatisfied for reasons I couldn't begin to understand. I couldn't figure out what was wrong with me.

Soon after the Promise Keepers event, I had lunch with my new friend Todd. He was a local businessman I had met at the prayer breakfast, very zealous for God and his church, and I think determined to win me over to the "right" side of which day to worship. More likely he was trying to help me move through my legalistic view of religion, the perceived code of Seventh-day Adventist conduct that many other followers of Christianity viewed as quite burdensome.

At any rate, I attempted to explain to him the change that had occurred in me—the undefined uneasiness and dissatisfaction I had felt since attending the Promise Keepers convention. I was unsettled and ready to experience something I could not at that time explain. I tried to share my experience with him and particularly my feeling of distance from what I had experienced as my "walk with God." I did my best to share that something very scary and also quite wonderful had happened. In spite of the uneasiness, I felt free, as if a heaviness had somehow been lifted.

I will never forget the look of horror on his face when my message eventually sunk in. His face took on a total lack of comprehension. I remember his discomfort as we said our goodbyes after lunch. I never heard from him again. He obviously was totally unable to understand how I could experience a spiritual transformation that would result in my separation from the church and religion.

My life has been a continual progression of my spiritual understanding since that day. It was not the end of my spirituality, but quite the opposite. My heart had indeed broken open at the Promise Keepers event. It's just that the results were not drawing me closer to organized religion; instead, my eyes were opening to the inconsistencies within the church and its belief system.

My search for understanding would eventually include an untidy divorce, "dis–memberment" from the Adventist church, and many painful years of searching.

It was then I discovered the "other person" in my head—the voice of my fear-mind: Dear Chester.

As I was discovering the existence of the fear-mind, I was introduced to the writings of Eckhart Tolle. That his writings appeared in my life at that particular time is an excellent example of the saying, "When the student is ready, the teacher will appear."

Several years ago, I was invited to ride along with my friend, Dave, to a chiropractic conference on beautiful Lake Chelan in eastern Washington.

It was a very busy time, and I remember being very motivated to create a change in my life. I had just sold my practice of seventeen years, and I was embarking on a new chapter in my profession. I was to become the donation director for a non-profit foundation, a task I was greatly anticipating. While I very much supported the goals of the foundation, I was more than a little nervous about the prospect of leaving a very good income for financial uncertainty.

When I hopped into Dave's car, I had several different things on my mind, and I was definitely not in a listening/receptive mode. Dave smiled his usual patient smile, shook my hand, said hello, and we headed off down the road toward our destination across the mountains. As we headed down the highway, I felt irritated by the voice of an audio book CD playing on his stereo. I asked Dave to turn it off, which he obligingly did for me without speaking. We arrived at the lake, ended up having a great weekend, learned a lot at the seminar, played in the lake, and all in all had a great time!

A couple of years later, I stumbled upon Eckhart Tolle's *The Power of Now*. I purchased the audio book and spent the next several weeks absolutely enthralled with Tolle's words and message about finding, living, and then staying in the "present moment" and hearing about the presence of a "voice in the head" or the fear-mind ego. I was so excited! Everyone I knew had to hear about this!

I am sure you can guess the rest of this story. The next time I spoke to Dave, I excitingly told him about the book and that he just had to get it and listen to it! NOW!

I recall my embarrassment when he calmly asked me whether I remembered our trip to Lake Chelan and then proceeded to explain that the CD he had been listening to was the same CD book, same author, and same teacher.

"When the student is ready, the teacher will appear." The teacher was there, but I, the student, was not ready. How many things did I need to learn the hard way? How much suffering is necessary to bring one to a point of surrender and to the foot of the path of enlightenment and awareness? As to the question "How much suffering is necessary?" Eckhart Tolle would say, "Whatever it takes is the amount that is necessary." If you, the student, are not ready today, Spirit will bring the lesson back into your life at another time. It may take a bit of discomfort or trauma in your life to get your attention, but it is helpful to remember that this pain is not punishment—it is an opportunity. You are not the victim of some arbitrary infliction; you are receiving a gift from Source. Do not throw it back in the face of universal intention! The next lesson may not be anywhere near as gentle!

I have been blessed with hard, dense bones. Sadly, my head is probably the densest bone of all! I sometimes complain that others seem to learn so much faster than me! I, for some reason, love to learn things the hard way. Maybe I should be grateful! Maybe the lessons I learn in this way have greater retention?

With my introduction to the "voice in my head," I had discovered the existence of my fear-mind. What Eckhart Tolle calls "the voice in the head," others have labeled the ego-self, ego-mind, or some other description. I do have that "voice in the head," and I have chosen to call it "Chester." I settled on the name Chester because the picture that came to me of the "person in my head" was of a comical trouble-maker—not unlike a court jester in the Middle Ages, complete with the three pronged hat, bells, upturned shoes, the whole bit. So the name Chester fit just fine.

Chester means well, but he is a troublemaker. He understands fear much like a fish understands water. He responds to and nurtures the language of fear. And the more he can engage me in his fear-based dramas, the more secure is his position. It's all about job security you know.

You can usually find Chester in the middle of a flurry of emotion, much like a dust devil in the center of a dry field. This cloud of emotion is created by Chester, and he is not satisfied until the tornado has grown to an intensity that all but obscures the centered Self.

Chester is in fine company. Just about every soul on this earth speaks the language of fear. Fear is the language of the unaware soul, the person totally identified with the fear-mind. Individually and collectively, we humans interact in fear, perhaps at different levels, but always at a huge expense to our well-being.

I believe we are essentially whole spiritual beings engaged in a physical experience. Our core nature is secure because innately we know we are connected to Source, by which I mean we innately know we are worthy and always connected to what the Native Americans call "Great Spirit." Nothing can threaten that knowing or connection except fear and the illusion of separation. And fear is simply an allowing of separation from our core being.

I picture my core being as a column of light that is tightly connected to Source. When identified with this core, I am in the present moment, in absolute joy of being and 100% present. All of my action and interaction is of positive spiritual motivation and the result is always beneficial.

Of course, I can experience a disconnection or separation from my Source. Fear, frustration, anger, pride, and many other illusory identifications with my fear-mind (Chester) can pull my being away from my core.

"The focus of our awareness becomes the reality of our world."
— **Gregg Braden**

When we allow our self to identify with the fear-mind, we reinforce our separateness and create opportunities for conflict with "the other." Chester knows he will always find a rational justification to go to war. Just look at all of our enemies! Those clueless unfortunates out there who are stupid enough to be on the wrong path! Whether it's the wrong church on the wrong day, or some misguided soul supporting the wrong political candidate, pursuing the wrong form of healthcare, praying to the wrong God! The list is endless.

How is it that we can so quickly pass judgment on another? Why can't we just as easily accept, support, and love our neighbor? One answer is that if our fear-mind can maintain our attention outside of our self, then Chester and the ego can be justified.

When we live outside of ourselves in the arena of ego control and fear-motivated action, our Chester will always have work to do. Judgment is easy when accountability is outside of one's self.

Wars will continue to rage and people will die to prove the side of right-ness or righteousness.

But this does not have to be! With awareness, the opportunity for change is here. With the dawn of personal consciousness comes an increasing gap between spiritual awareness and the darkness of fear.

Will we, with our spiritual absence, allow Chester to continue his warfare? Or will our awareness keep Chester quiet and under control? We can only make the choice if we have the level of awareness to understand a choice exists. Dealing with Chester is a bit like asking your four year old whether he wants vegetables or ice cream for dinner. If given a choice, the fear-mind will always choose conflict over peace.

One of my favorite movies is *Castaway* with Tom Hanks. In a very powerful scene at the movie's end, Tom Hanks' character is standing at the intersection of two country roads, with four options to take. He turns slowly in the middle of the intersection and looks intently down each of the four roads, each representing a path to a different destiny in life. His last lingering look is down the road that the beautiful redhead has just driven down. The romantic in me chooses to believe he followed the girl. But the bigger question is...could he make the "best" decision without having gone through the challenges portrayed earlier in the movie? Would he even have brought himself to that point of choice at all? Our life experience and journey is one of awakening. We are bringing challenges and opportunities into our lives for the very purpose of setting the stage for choice. Conscious choice. In my understanding, choice is not an option of the spiritually comatose.

This is our "work." To raise awareness, to share the "good news" with our fellow travelers. To understand that we lack "nothing" because we are spiritually and emotionally complete!

This paradigm sort of messes with the mission of the church. What would happen if people in large numbers understood that their only "sin" was unconsciousness? Religion teaches people that they are basically flawed. For people to awaken to the understanding that they are complete and whole spiritual beings would unravel the agenda of many fear-based organizations.

My boys love to play chess, Chinese checkers, and Monopoly. To complete any one of those games, there must be a winner and a loser. Similarly, in the "game" of the fear-mind life, someone must win and someone must lose. But what would happen if we chose not to play by that game and realized the insanity of that system? What if the only reality were that we are all winners and we are all innately complete and lack for nothing? What could organized religion do with people who attained and accepted an observation of self that transcended the belief system of the church?

I think we all know the answer to that hypothetical question. The current religion-based belief systems would disappear overnight. The new "church" would be a community of people celebrating life and spirit, a group of people all too rare in the ecclesiastical circles of today. The lure of church based on the paradigm of "sin" and incompleteness would have to be replaced with a system that acknowledged the basic spiritual completeness of the human soul.

Let's get back to Chester for a moment. Who is this guy anyway?

Chester (my chosen name for the fear-mind) is that image of you that is lonely, fearful, paranoid, and insecure. It helps me to picture Chester as a sort of hand puppet. He only becomes animated when we put him on, or give him "life" if you will. Otherwise, when quietly observed, he assumes a rather limp posture and is pretty much helpless and harmless.

If you are a parent, you may appreciate my experience with children in my chiropractic office. I have found that almost without exception when I have children acting out as patients, they are feeding on their parents' fear and uncertainty. Children are usually innately trusting and quite intelligent. But because of their trusting natures, they will accept and take on the fear and insecurity of their parents. They learn well and fast.

So when I have a small patient unnecessarily acting out, rather than look at the child, I direct my focus on the parent and deal with that. Then the out-of-control child calms right down (usually!).

Many questions I had about my life finally clicked place for me when I was able to see a distinction between my ego mind/self and my Source self. I was unable to achieve any intellectual grasp or objective view of the fear-mind until I perceived (created) the gap of separation. Up to that time, I was fully and constantly identified with my "fear" self, my ego self. When I realized this distinction and was able to observe this fear-actuated self, it all made sense. It was then I named this other self "Chester." I finally understood that my "salvation" lay completely in observing the comic antics of poor Chester.

Eternally with his foot in his mouth, the proverbial bull in the china shop, that's my beloved Chester. Quick to make assumptions, and lightning quick to defend and punish were all skills I observed in Chester. You may ask, "Why didn't you just give Chester the boot?" Well, that is hard to do when I am the culprit. Chester is the summation of my ego defense and identity. To kill Chester would be to kill me. "Doctor, the operation was a success but sadly the patient died."

Remember the old *Star Trek* episode where our hero Captain Kirk went through the faulty transporter (way to go Scotty!) then emerged at his destination physically separate from his Ego? That was a fine bit of writing in that episode! The landing party was beaming aboard the *Enterprise* when the transporter accidentally split the captain from his ego self. When Captain Jim (I can't remember if he still had his shirt on or not) eventually realized his predicament, he also understood that to destroy his Ego self would also destroy its complementary self. So the only way out was to merge with/reconnect with his ego, his "Chester." The portrayal of Captain Kirk, *sans* ego, was very graphic. What emerged was a picture of a spineless wimp, indecisive, weak, and uncertain. This is the portrayal Chester wants you to see. "Without me, you are nothing! Weak! Easy prey to any and all who seek to destroy you/us!" However, this is where I think the *Star Trek* writers got the concept wrong. In reality, without the ego in control, we can learn to be even stronger.

Chester is a bit limited in the intelligence department. He does not understand the difference between force and power. In the book *Power vs. Force*, David Hawkins perfectly describes the disparity and differences between the qualities of power and force. Power does not need to be defended by the ego. Force, on the other hand, must be constantly fed with fear-mind energy. Force manipulates, where power allows. Force tears down, while power supports. Force is noisy and abrasive; power is silent and uplifting in spiritual energy. Our ego mind is inconsistent with power and yet equated with force. Power is magnetic; force is repellent.

Do you remember what it was like when you were attracted to the love of your life? How much force did you use? If your mate is anything like mine, force was not only unhelpful, but very counterproductive in the wooing department!

Listening

I promised my wife I would include a section on the value of listening and how it has changed, and continues to change, my life. I wonder why she suggested that?

Many people definitely struggle with the art of listening, often giving an appearance of attention, which is usually a thinly veiled attempt to wait for an opportunity to speak. Chester doesn't like to sit quietly for anything or anyone. So listening can be a big problem.

The most beautiful gift you can give another is the gift of conscious listening. If you can separate yourself from the needs of your fear-mind long enough to be present, the reward is priceless. However, if you acquiesce to the tactlessness of Chester, you will very likely miss the opportunity to connect with another and embarrass yourself in the process.

During a wonderful retreat my wife and I attended on the island of Molokai in Hawaii, our facilitator, Bob, led us in a sharing session, giving each of us an opportunity to share a short story and its life lesson for us.

Talk about performance anxiety! I desperately searched my memory cells for an appropriate story. My primary intent was to impress the circle with its relevance and impact.

I was so busy with this task I wasn't paying much attention to the speaking and sharing going on around me. Several people spoke, and I vaguely recall Bob telling a story that was received with rapt attention by most of the group. Good thing they were entertained because I couldn't be bothered! I was determined to find the perfect story and impress everyone with my brilliance!

Then it was my turn! My chance! Thankfully, I had stumbled upon a story I had previously read about the true experience of the writer of the song "Amazing Grace."

I launched into the short and rather stumbling narration of my version of this man's experience. John Newton, a ship captain, was relieved at the ship's wheel by another sailor who was washed overboard only seconds later. Newton steered the ship through the remainder of the storm, and during that experience, underwent a conversion, realizing his helplessness and that only the grace of God could save him. The familiar hymn, "Amazing Grace," was written from this experience.

I noticed as I spoke, even though primarily focused on my own discomfort and fear, that people were giving each other sidelong glances and for some reason trying to be polite. With horror, I soon realized my story was the same story earlier related by my friend Bob.

I embarrassingly apologized when I learned of my *faux pas* and somehow endured the rest of the evening. I will never forget the depth of my embarrassment. Fortunately, Bob graciously forgave me and we did end up laughing about it later.

Melanie continually yet gently reminds me of the virtues of listening. I am grateful for this experience for it helped to remind me of the folly of giving less than optimal attention and not listening when others have the floor. To have this happen in front of my peers was indeed terribly embarrassing, and I am sure it was a very powerful lesson for them as well. But at my expense.

Darn that Chester guy! He sure gets me into a lot of trouble!

Entitlement

Chester loves to show off his shiny suit of armor and clomp around the castle trying to prove how important he is. The more he can enhance his sense of self, the more secure he feels.

One of his particularly obnoxious traits is his feeling of entitlement, his belief that his egoistic self must be advanced at the expense of service to others.

What is the healthy difference between a conscious acknowledgment of our divine nature and the negative aspects of entitlement? At what point is that line crossed?

I believe it all comes back to whether our self is identified with Chester (ego) or with Source.

I recently witnessed someone experiencing a lesson in entitlement. I had just begun to feel comfortable letting a young doctor I had hired in my practice see patients on his own. He had become familiar with the intricacies of our X-ray department and with the office so my office manager agreed he was ready for that responsibility.

The evening before his first day on his own, because I knew he had previously been employed as a computer technician and programmer, I asked him to give a hand if needed to our computer man who was coming the next day to install a new network server. He agreed and I happily drove off feeling confident and thankful that I now had someone I could trust with my "baby," my practice.

The next morning, as is my habit, I was up early checking e-mails before heading off to do a few errands. To my surprise, I opened a rather strongly worded message from my new associate, informing me that under no circumstances would he make himself available as "my computer guy." I was a bit surprised by his tone, feeling justified that I had not taken advantage of him since I was paying my computer man to do the work and had only asked the new doc to give a hand if necessary.

The doctor went on to say that he had not gone through eight years of chiropractic college to be my "computer guy" at a measly amount of money.

Well, he didn't last the morning in my office. I calmly (thanks for sittin' this one out, Chester!) explained to him that one of the first things I was told by Dr. Rodney, twenty-two years earlier (my first experience in a clinical setting outside of chiropractic college), was that if I were too important to clean out a plugged up toilet or sweep the floors, then I was likely in the wrong profession.

Service and entitlement, an inflated sense of importance and ego, do not mix well.

This young doctor had definitely learned an important lesson. After he had calmed down, he e-mailed me a couple of days later to ask for my forgiveness, which of course I assured him he had, but it was apparent we were not meant to work together. I am thankful I learned about his Chester earlier than later.

At the risk of sounding like an old codger, "What is going on with this new generation?"

Of course, this attitude is nothing new and this "new generation" is probably no guiltier of entitlement issues than any generation before, but it seems that way!

Our country feels entitled to continue to kill in response to September 11. "Never forget" is the watchword. Actually, "Never forgive" seems more accurate. The tragedy of 9/11 was a terrible expression of egoistic aggression on a grand scale, but our national response elevated a tragedy into a war of global proportions that will take generations to heal. If only George Bush and his advisors had taken time to reflect on what each of their Chesters was capable of doing and instead maintained human decency and spiritual accountability, a lot of pain and suffering could have been prevented.

"There is no distinctly native American criminal class...
save Congress."
— Mark Twain

Chester must have his revenge. The old saying, "When embarking on a mission of revenge, first dig two graves" is very appropriate. Revenge does not heal.

Imagine two kindergarten schools in a nice neighborhood. A child from one school decides to wander over to the other school to whack some poor unsuspecting kid on the head with a stick. Would the appropriate response be to issue bigger sticks to all the "offended" kids and encourage them to run over and beat the crap out of the other school's constituents? Where is the wisdom, let alone spiritual maturity of that?

Remember Robert Fulghum's book *All I Really Need to Know I Learned in Kindergarten*? Those important lessons included, "Clean up after yourself," "Say I'm sorry," and "Give a helping hand."

Why is it our collective Chester must kill and persecute in response to injury? Why is it that the elected leader of the free world does not possess even the most basic moral attributes of a kindergartner?

We have an opportunity to awaken to a higher order and level of spiritual living. Or, it could go the other way—we are in no way entitled to survive as a human race. We have the opportunity to destroy ourselves with fear and revenge. Fortunately, we also have the opportunity to work through this challenge of identity. Are we Chester? Or is Chester merely an out-of-control expression of ego self, our fear-mind?

There are many signs in the world that spirit is awakening. There is increased interest in what used to be termed "New Age," and fortunately, we are seeing more and more of these "New Age" authors, more widely accepted now and termed "spiritual" being published and read by a wider and wider range of audience. This increasing interest in spirituality is a sure sign that people are awakening to their power and casting aside the fear that has held them back or made them act irrationally. The grip of the conservative fear-based consciousness is loosening on a global scale. The "bad news" is that as spirit awakens, the collective Chester gets more uncomfortable. As the collective fear-mind sees its power being eroded, the craziness of fear is becoming bolder.

Need an example of this? Turn on your radio or television and listen for a few minutes.

To further the awakening of spirit, turn your television off. Don't give in to the collective fear-mind any longer but trust your spirit, listen to it, and act accordingly.

"There would be nothing to frighten you if you refused to be afraid."
— Gandhi

6

TAMING CHESTER

"A slip of the foot you may soon recover, but a slip of the tongue you may never get over."
— **Benjamin Franklin**

I have always tended to be a bit of a crusader. Things have appeared either black or white to me. There is a right way and a wrong way. You are either on the side of righteousness or on the slippery slope to ruin. It can be a heavy load to carry. My wife gets tired just looking at me.

Several years ago, I attended a seminar given by my classmate and friend, Dr. Eric Plasker. Dr. Eric is quite a dynamo and has a talent for attracting the best and brightest in our chiropractic profession to his seminars. For this seminar, he had invited Dr. Roger Turner of Toronto, Canada. Dr. Turner had made a name for himself by developing a technique of adjusting the cranium. This by itself was fuel for my skepticism. Of course everyone knows the sutures of the skull are fused, so claiming to adjust the skull's segments was fanciful at best, and at worst—well, all we need is another chiropractor feeding fuel to our profession's critics.

To this day, Dr. Turner chuckles with me when he recalls our first meeting. He remembers watching me standing with arms crossed, impolitely glaring across the seminar room, my body language telling everyone around me what I thought of this guy.

To put my behavior here in perspective, let me explain how I achieved such a practiced level of intolerance. Years earlier, while president of the student government at Life Chiropractic College, I had tried to rid the campus and student body of what I considered the dangerous teaching of a technique faction in chiropractic called the neuro-organizational technique, or N.O.T. This technique was boldly proclaiming that subtle misalignments of the cranium, sacrum, and other less visited sites in the human body could be the cause of many emotional, psychological, and other physical ills. After I proclaimed that this technique was "not chiropractic," I proceeded to purge the campus of the unfortunate students and faculty who were un- wise enough to associate with this "cult." Fortunately, my crusade was largely ineffective and the crisis gradually dissipated.

Years later, Dr. Turner used a great deal of N.O.T. to formulate his cranial adjusting technique.

Then I reappeared on the scene. I was a bit alarmed at the presence of Dr. Turner at such a professional gathering as Dr. Plasker's event. How could Dr. Eric invite someone like that to this seminar? Wow, the standards sure were slipping! I stood there for probably two hours watching a long line of doctors, family members, and students submit to his analysis and then the cranial adjustment.

My wife suggested I walk over, introduce myself, and get adjusted to see for myself what it was all about. I looked at her like she was insane, and declined. The next day was the same. More people, many more people, moved through the line as Dr. Turner patiently explained and demonstrated his procedures and technique.

This was crazy! What was he saying to them? Finally, I could stand it no longer so I got in line. I figured the worst he could do was waste my time, and maybe I could talk some sense into him.

His smile was huge when I finally got to the front of the line. I apparently wasn't the only one observing that weekend. He didn't say much, just proceeded to examine my neck and then palpate my head. I submitted to the neck adjustment while mutely criticizing every move. Then he proceeded to check and adjust my head.

Most chiropractors at that time believed the skull's plates were fused and immovable in adults. I was to learn differently.

Not only did my head get an adjustment—so did my mental perspective!

I spent the balance of that weekend feeling like my head was the size of a warehouse. Some of my friends would probably say that wasn't much of a stretch, but from my point of view, my life had changed! Not only could I feel my head occupying new space, but my belief systems had been significantly challenged and transformed. To say I was impressed and humbled is an understatement.

The next week I flew to Calgary, Alberta to attend Dr. Turner's next seminar. What I witnessed and experienced there changed my life. I felt with my hands things that I would have sworn were impossible.

One lady brought in her twelve-year old son who had been imprisoned in a wheelchair his entire life. Totally unable to speak, he was unable even to hold eye contact with those around him. His mother had the patient, tired look that only a twenty-four hour a day caregiver can develop. She looked hopeful, but she obviously wasn't expecting too much. Dr. Turner spent about half an hour examining the young man before giving him an adjustment. I admired his persistence and daring and the quiet confidence that only someone with his level of knowing could display.

Within minutes of the examination and correction, the boy in the chair started vocalizing. Not speaking, but making grunts and obvious efforts at communication. When his eyes locked onto Dr. Turner's, I could see the non-verbal communication occurring. His mother broke down in tears and shared that for the first time in his life he was focusing on another person's eyes and vocalizing.

This event changed me as well. My belief in the limits of cranial work had been seriously challenged and blown away. Once again, my criticism and narrow-minded perspective had been shown for what they were—illusion based in fear.

I have since witnessed tremendous results with the cranial adjusting technique in my practice. Headaches with decades of duration have disappeared in my patients. Visual and auditory disorders have improved. Some cases of seizure activity have responded very favorably. Patients with conditions resistant to spinal adjustments were responding well with the addition of the cranial adjustments.

My mind had indeed expanded, not only for my benefit but my patients as well.

Like Saul persecuting the biblical Christians, my error in judgment and criticisms had been brought to light. It had come full circle. The very technique I had criticized and persecuted twenty-five years before in school had been introduced to me again in the form of a very valuable lesson. I was indeed humbled. And I am thankful for the lesson I had served myself.

I now feel honored to be called Dr. Turner's friend and professional associate. I receive referrals from him here in Seattle, and of course, I recommend him and his work highly. Apparently, you can teach an old dog new tricks. I now observe myself more carefully, and I am much less apt to criticize, preferring not to catch myself in a critical attitude for any reason. Chester does his best to lure me into criticism and attack, but he does not succeed in his subterfuge for long. I grow more familiar with his tricks and techniques with each attempt.

When you give yourself the opportunity to observe how this fear mechanism works, it can be quite comical. After all, remember I equate Chester's antics with those of a court jester.

"The energy field of old but still very-much-alive emotion that lives in almost every human being is the pain-body.
The pain-body, however, is not just individual in nature.
It also partakes of the pain suffered by countless humans throughout the history of humanity."
— Eckhart Tolle

A Stool For Chester

With help from Eckhart Tolle's The Power of Now, I realized part of me fed on fear, much like a vampire feeds on fear and blood. With this new perspective, I was able to observe Chester, the part of me creating so much pain.

But what to do with the little fella? It was too dangerous to let him run amuck. As always, the answer came through observation.

To understand my internal dynamic, I drew a mental picture of my spiritual Self and Chester in the "throne room" of my mind. I created a nice comfy stool for Chester to sit on, and I placed it in a corner where I could easily observe him. I knew keeping a watchful eye on the guy was the key to figuring out how to handle him. And as time passed, I began to see he was really quite clever.

My first few weeks observing Chester on his stool were without doubt the most enlightening experience of my life. It was fascinating as well as a bit scary. The emerging freedom achieved by observing my other "self" explained much concerning my painful journey to that point.

Watching Chester twitch and squirm when a car cut in front of me on the freeway, when a patient had the nerve to cancel an appointment, or when my wife left a cupboard door hanging open (I know; pretty sad, isn't it?) was very enlightening. The quiet power and peace of mind obtained through the space of observance was absolutely transforming.

But then Chester got smart. As I observed, he adapted. A few weeks into this experiment, I noticed some old irritations, sources of anger and intolerance, begin to resurface. I still had a lot to learn about Chester, and whenever I took my attention from him, he would show me he was still as active as ever.

Most of the time Chester gave the appearance of innocent docility, and when I looked in his direction, his funny three-cornered hat was just where I had last seen it, his form slouched in the now familiar pose of thinly disguised resignation.

It took me a couple of days to realize Chester had cleverly planted a double and sneaked around behind me! I had failed to remember that Chester (ego) equates his deactivation or taming with death itself! So any method of trickery was fair game!

As the game played on, I quickly realized my calm, constant observance of Chester was essential for any chance of continued peace and joy in my life. Chester was constantly ready to pick a fight, but as I grew in understanding, I realized I must get to a point where he could not get under my skin. We had to learn to live together, to merge into a seamless "whole" once again. Since the fear-mind and ego are part of us, we will never be able to eliminate Chester completely from our lives, nor would we want to. Our Ego-reactive self is a useful tool to have in an emergency. It is, however, a tool best left in the tool chest when not needed. For example, a sharp knife is a useful tool when the situation is appropriate, but best left in the drawer when giving your spouse a hug!

Your ego mind can assist you in very specific tasks under the watchful eye of your observance. This can be done without identifying with fear and creating drama.

Now when Chester gets restless, I observe him and then send him to his corner to do community service or write, "I am…" statements. Sure, he grumbles no end, but his attention is diverted from engaging self to the gift of giving. Hundreds of "I am loving" statements written in longhand are enough to bring even the most obnoxious Chester to his knees.

By observing your fear-mind, your Chester, you are reclaiming your ability to create joy in your life. When identified with Chester, you are again a victim, tossed about by external events.

When Chester sticks his nose in and presents the opportunity to engage in fear, our choice or response instead could be "Thank you, Chester! I will take that under advisement."

By remembering that the fear-mind is an essential, though overused tool, we can appreciate the positive qualities of our fear-mind without agreeing with the path that leads to paralysis and more fear generation.

Observe. Take the information from Chester under advisement. This will, in time, reduce the impact of the fear-mind in your life.

"Fear is the cheapest room in the house.
I would like to see you living in better conditions."
— Hafiz

Comfort Zone

Chester has a comfort zone. He is happiest when there is a base level of drama and conflict keeping him busy. If things get quiet, which will occur with your basic observation, he gets very nervous and will do his best to stir things up.

Many people will keep a television or radio on to help keep mind activity going. Silence makes them uncomfortable. Chester, with the support of our current, fear-based culture, is primarily responsible for this need. Studies performed for the advertising industry calculated the optimal rates of visual and auditory stimulation for the best effect in modifying behavior. The fast, constantly moving images on the video screen are no mistake; nor are they the result of a video cameraman with Parkinson's. They are calculated for a very specific effect: Control. And Chester is their target. Consequently, your ability to regain control of your mind and consciousness is a direct threat to the current agenda of consumerism and the orchestrated agenda of political will.

Sounds a bit paranoid. Or maybe just "perrynoid." A favorite movie of mine is Conspiracy Theory, starring Mel Gibson and Julia Roberts. Gibson plays a cab driver in New York City who is convinced the government is actively controlling his life and those of everyone in the country. He is initially viewed as crazy, until a series of events convinces people otherwise. Of course, it's just a movie, but even the products of Hollywood can be insightful.

Our political system depends on the unconsciousness of the average American citizen. Consciousness and accountability in the individual citizen necessarily calls for integrity and accountability in government. Sounds a bit cynical, but consciousness is the last thing big government and special interest corporate America wants. They survive on the comatose, Chester-induced reactivity of the general population. With each step an individual takes toward awareness and personal accountability, the foundation of government control is weakened. We reclaim the freedom that is our constitutional right.

So continue to do whatever you can to weaken and intimidate Chester's level of comfort. Hold him in the light of your awareness. He is pretty much a wimp in this position. But still a bit dangerous. Keep your eyes open for his inevitable attempt at regaining control and the upper hand.

Take active steps to create an environment that is nourishing to your spiritual mind while also being a threat to the control of Chester. Make your home a spiritual oasis. Luxuriate in silence and beauty. Do what you can to minimize noise and chaos in your personal space.

While I have tried to allow and respect the current trend in art, music, and popular culture that glorifies noise and random action, I cannot bring myself to appreciate it. Music that assaults the senses and stimulates an adrenaline response in the absence of any real threat cannot contribute to spiritual connection. With the growth in spiritual presence comes a corresponding intolerance of fear-generated noise.

We have entered an age where authentic beauty in music, architecture, and art are increasingly difficult to find. Is it a coincidence that correspondingly we see crises in the areas of religion, politics, and economics? Where is the connection between nourishing spiritual soundness and allowing Chester to bounce off the walls?

Create your "happy place." Guard with diligence the environment that supports your spiritual intention and journey. Reconnect with the value of immersing yourself in nature and low-tech pursuits. Take a walk in the woods, a drive to the mountains. Be okay with silence and quiet. Depending on how entrenched Chester is in your mind identity, it may take quite a bit of time and perseverance, but I know you can do it. You will appreciate the return to your authentic self. Put Chester on notice. The gig's up!

Try not to be intimidated by the enormity of the task. Every step you take in the direction of spiritual peace will be rewarded with a growing sense of joy. You have everything you need to assure your success in this endeavor. Don't let Chester convince you otherwise.

"Whether you think you can or you think you can't, you're right."
— Henry Ford

Abundance

I was raised to believe the only way you obtain anything of value is through hard work. Knowing the value of hard work is a blessing, but for me, with that blessing came the belief, reinforced by Chester, that abundance is limited and only available through a harsh system of exchange. Chester will convince you the only way to bring abundance into your experience is through great effort.

Chester's thinking is a bit twisted. Fear dictates that there is never enough so we must strive very hard and with much pain to "get" what we need in order to survive. And that often can mean taking from others since there isn't enough to go around—precisely why our egos propel humans into fighting wars.

This focus on lack of abundance is typical propaganda from my dear Chester. Mix a little bit of falsehood in a large quantity of truth and the result is deception in its most subtle form. The good things are in short supply; to get what you need, you have to work hard, and too bad if you have to step on someone else to get what is rightfully yours!

Focusing on "hard work" keeps the language of fear out of your consciousness, but it remains in your subconscious. It is hard to identify and overcome because we have become so accustomed to living in that fear. We are conditioned to speaking fear's language.

"People who consider themselves victims of their circumstances will always remain victims unless they develop a greater vision for their lives."
— Stedman Graham, speaker, author, and educator

If you invite fear into your thoughts, life will continue to support you by giving you opportunities to overcome fear.

This is the Law of Attraction.

My experience with fear is that it slams shut the door through which abundance flows. The vibrational energy of fear is inconsistent with the attractive energy of abundance. Lack is a direct result of fear consciousness, so focusing on lack will only perpetuate the challenge of lack.

"The money I have is in direct proportion to the value I've given to others. The more I give of myself, incredibly, the more economic power comes my way."
— **Tod Barnhart, author**

Esther and Jerry Hicks, in their book The Law of Attraction, describe beautifully how this universal law works. We manifest into our lives exactly what we vibrate, with intention, out into the universal "web." The scary part of the Law of Attraction is that it works. Period. We can and will attract by default, always in response to the level of our emotional vibration. If we are resonating in fear, we attract those experiences into our lives that support and create fear. If we transmit love, peace, joy, and acceptance into the web, we will manifest the fruit of these qualities. There are no exceptions. It is a law that works as surely and efficiently as gravity.

With intention comes the opportunity to change the course of our lives and experiences. And with awareness and knowledge of this universal law comes a freedom to create exactly what we want to see in our lives.

Many people seem to experience abundance effortlessly. Sadly, attracting abundance has not been my experience most of my life. For some reason, I made the process difficult, and because I grew up not knowing the rules of the game, I created by default. My experience was purchased with the unit of exchange I had learned to use. Fear.

Fear only buys more fear. But anxiety also attracts more opportunities to work through that belief system. This creates a cycle that will build until we create a sufficient crisis to blow us out of our fear-induced coma. So as you interact with money, if you are in reaction every time, you will be challenged by this fear and thereby create and attract more uncomfortable situations until you learn your lesson.

"If you look at what you have in life, you'll always have more. If you look at what you don't have in life, you'll never have enough."
— Oprah Winfrey

We have shown up in this physical life to experience and express. What would the experience be like if there were no challenge, no opportunity for growth? From Chester's point of view, great! From the standpoint of our essential Self, how boring!

Can you imagine how pointless a Super Bowl game would be with no challenges for the offensive team? Where is the fun in that? I believe our spiritual Self has created purpose in this life through the challenges that engage us. We are presented with opportunities to experience, grow, and be challenged. However, Chester will likely interpret all of this from the victim's viewpoint. Any uninvited challenge is perceived as a tribulation from God, persecution from Satan, or at the very least just bad luck. Chester views the challenge as something to be avoided, not a learning experience.

Chester cannot even begin to understand any level of accountability to that degree. He lives in the ultimate bastion of the "home of the blame." Without someone to blame, his purpose for being in control would be gone. He would be relegated back to his useful role as the "go-to guy" in case of real emergency.

Our identification with our ego, fear-mind self is what has gotten us stuck. We have let Chester call the plays. It is time to put Chester back on the "special teams" bench where he belongs!

We live in an abundant universe. The problem arises when our neediness expects material things to complete us and make us whole again.

Spending more than one makes is probably one of the most self-destructive habits in our society. This expression of fear not only creates a great deal of stress, but it also radiates fear into every corner of your life. The toll on relationships is immense.

How do we create debt? Beyond the obvious answer of spending more than we receive, what are the mind patterns and belief systems that lead to this addiction, this form of fear?

Debt is an expression of fear. Fear of not having enough. Fear that for some reason we are not complete unless we possess something outside of self. A thing, that when obtained, will lead to a feeling or belief that we are safe and secure.

Believe me, I understand from a personal experiential level how destructive debt can be. I learned some bad habits early in life in the area of finances. My belief system of lack soon created a mind-set that I must "get" and have at any cost. The resulting burden of debt was soon crippling and extended well into my adult life. I am still dealing with the reverberations of this learned behavior. What has had to occur is a complete rewriting of my belief system concerning worthiness and security. And it has not been easy. In fact, the effects of debt on my personal life have been one of my biggest challenges.

Debt creates a vibrational energy that has a very potent negative effect on the universe's positive attractive forces. Debt blocks the abundance that is ours to experience. It blinds us to the very real existence of abundance that is inherent in every atom and fiber of our physical experience.

Chester supports the fear that leads to this consciousness of lack and the experience of debt. If Chester is not controlled with our awareness, his fear will attract an ongoing lesson of debt in our lives.

The Building Storm: The Dark Night of the Soul

As awareness of the fear-mind's insanity builds, Chester becomes more desperate for control and acknowledgment as your mental king. Where once there was sneakiness and craft, now a brutal force is struggling to regain dominance.

The fantasy is that with awareness and enlightenment, our days will be filled with sunshine and flowers, relationships will be easy, and personal struggles a thing of the past. However, the stereotype of the peaceful, enlightened monk, smiling angelically while calmly enjoying his existence, is an illusion.

The monk has hemorrhoids. His wife is unreasonable, his kids rebellious and irresponsible. The sought after Shangri-La is found to be another deception of the ego.

The truth is, life sucks. Your socks still get holes in them, your garden still grows weeds, and you still have to take out the garbage. What is even more noticeable is the dramatic range of the highs and the lows. Of particular notice, as awareness of Chester increases, is that the lows really are low!

This is the "dark night of the soul." Chester expresses a viciousness that was unnecessary earlier when you were ensconced in your peaceful coma of existence. Desperate times for Chester necessitate desperate measures. He takes on a dark and brooding countenance, his armor turning a malevolent shade of slate gray. This is both painful to experience and also an opportunity to be met with much gratitude.

There is some good news, however. True, the lows are low, but you will have moved to a new position of perspective. What you now perceive as a low is actually a much higher plane when perceived from heightened consciousness.

As I have said, once awareness is experienced, there is no turning back. The luxury of existing in the comatose state is no longer a viable alternative. Once you recognize Chester for who he is, and once he knows that you know, the gloves come off. The transformation has begun, and once set in motion, nothing can impede its progress.

Books that once entertained now no longer hold an appeal. Once favorite television shows now appear simply idiotic. The forms of escape that before were havens of refuge are no longer attractive. There is no longer the excuse of unconsciousness to hide behind. The momentary slip of the fear-mind and reaction is immediately recognized and put back under control.

Without dedicated attention, this change can be quite painful. It is important you remain focused on your goals: Awareness, understanding, and enlightenment. Now is the time to live in spiritual integrity. You must remember that Chester is fighting for his life. Any opportunity he sees as a chance to reignite indignation, anger, or righteousness is an opportunity, no matter how slim the chance. All you have to do is open the door of invitation just a crack and Chester is all over the opportunity.

Myth says that when Lucifer was banished from Heaven, he was condemned to earth as his domain. He was destined to an eternity of attempts to re-establish his claim on human consciousness. He is said to be brilliant and cunning. He has nothing to lose and everything to gain. No scheme is beneath him. Any means justifies the end. I now see the connection of this allegory to the working of the fear-based ego-mind and my Chester. The devil really did make me do it! Are there horns hiding under that tri-colored hat with bells?

If you feel you must believe in a literal, external Satan, understand that he is not down in some sulphuric hell somewhere. That may work for Hollywood and Sunday School, but let's rise a bit to a level of accountability here. If you allow Satan's existence, realize he exists in your fear-mind consciousness. Understand that any base human action or thought is within your capability. Few people are willing to accept this level of spiritual and moralistic accountability. Satan is Chester, and Chester is Satan. And that is not necessarily a derogatory comment on Chester. The important question here is "Whom will you identify with?" Fear-identified Satan or an intentionally free spiritual and moral agent with creative license. With which reality will you establish an agreement?

I discovered a higher level of accountability when I realized I contained within myself the same potential for evil as any Hitler, Idi Amin, Osama bin Laden, or Attila the Hun. I am no better and no worse. The greatest good and the lowest evil are not "out there somewhere" waiting to be bestowed or ready to pounce. I am utterly responsible and dependent on my level of identification with the fear-mind and its demands for justice and revenge. With this understanding comes a huge measure of humility, compassion (for myself and others), and a desire for change and watchfulness in my life.

Chester may be cute at times, but his potential is incredibly vicious and not to be underestimated. This is not an awareness to be feared. That would again be a foothold for ego and an ongoing cycle of fear-based action and reaction. Like the cute little animals in the movie Gremlins, once provoked and threatened, there is no limit to the evil that can potentially be released. Chester the Court Jester will transform into Chester the "Dark Knight."

The battle with this Dark Knight is the dark night of the soul, a long dark night of despair, unless with awareness, courage, intention, and attention, Chester is pacified and disciplined with observance. So how does one deal with the "Dark Knight" when he jumps off his corner stool, sword blazing, ready for battle?

Vigilance. By paying attention to and heeding the messages from Spirit. Esther Hicks, in the Teachings of Abraham, refers to these messages as the "emotional guidance system." Very simple. "Good feelings" indicate harmony with spirit. "Bad feelings" indicate dis-harmony with Spirit. Of course, my religious friends get very nervous when I speak about this—how can you rely on feelings in matters of integrity and morality?

Just before my divorce, I was struggling to understand what I was feeling and where I felt my life was heading. My wife and I had traveled to Georgia to visit my college friend Steve and his new wife Sally. I remember sitting in Steve's car talking as we headed to the store on an errand. I had risked sharing with Steve my feelings, my uncertainty about staying married, and my newfound hunger for things spiritual and not religious.

His counsel was firm and definite. "You can't trust your feelings. They will only get you into trouble." I understood where he was coming from because he felt he had lost his first wife because she had followed her feelings.

But how could I not trust my feelings? Were they inherently bad? Where did they come from? This was new territory for me. I had trusted the rules all my life. And how safe had that turned out to be? My whole life had been a hard push up a steep hill. Where was the happiness, the joy, the freedom? Is life just to be endured? Following the rules hadn't made me safe, so how could listening to my feelings be such a danger? Was it really true that life is hell, so just wait for heaven?

That scenario no longer resonated with me. The old assurances of safety, salvation, and eternal peace somewhere beyond Orion's belt no longer floated my boat. Something was pulling me toward the brink. My intuition beckoned me to step off the edge. And I did.

I decided to trust my feelings.

During my divorce, I was privileged to make the acquaintance of an excellent relationship therapist, Wayne. Today, I believe Wayne's role in my life was to help me ask questions, although at the time, all I wanted was answers.

I remember asking Wayne, "What is the purpose of relationships?" I was disheartened by the illusion of safety the church and marriage provided. I can still see his slow grin, infuriating at the time, as I desperately asked these and other heart-wrenching questions.

Back then, it was all about me. What can I get out of a relationship? What can this person do for me? Now I realize an intimate relationship is an opportunity and license to learn. Tolle shares that a relationship's ultimate blessing is the spiritual environment it provides for personal and spiritual growth. I sure wish someone had shared that page of the manual with me thirty plus years ago. I was privileged to find this out the hard way, and I am still learning!

Feelings count. If we fear them and make them wrong, we discount the most valid indicator of our connection with our true self, our Source. By dismissing our feelings, we rely on the fear-induced indicators of our fear-mind. Chester and the fear-mind are constantly thinking in the language and art of fear, generating thoughts that keep us in reactive mode. If we allow Chester free rein, the onslaught of fear-generated thoughts will never cease. So the logical conclusion to prevent constant mental havoc is we must constantly monitor and guard our thoughts.

But this is impossible. Constantly guarding your thoughts is exhausting and ineffective. You cannot possibly monitor, judge, and guard against your thoughts. The results can only be frustration, guilt, and eventual hopelessness. Thinking with the calculating, fearful mind is Chester's forte. Feelings are the language of Spirit.

If a feeling of dissatisfaction surfaces, place your attention and focus on its source. Is the feeling the result of fear-created imagination? Is Chester causing trouble due to your absence? Is he whispering words of fear, entitlement, justice, or righteousness in your ear? If he is, how and why was he given the opportunity?

This area is where an unobserved fear-mind will create the most damage. If Chester is allowed dominance, replacing your centered, observing Self with his fear-based presence, your feelings definitely cannot be trusted. Feelings are authentic and can be your best indicator of consciousness unless you have allowed yourself to slide backwards into the fear-controlled mind.

Let your awareness of the troublemaker Chester defuse the situation at its source and return him to silence, before your reaction engages and the fight begins. Try not to make this more difficult than it needs to be. Use your feelings and pain productively; let them direct you toward opportunities of understanding and awareness of your Chester.

Remember to give yourself a break and view yourself with compassion. Chester wants you to fight and make this journey of awakening difficult. Be. Breathe. Stay flexible.

And don't forget to have some fun.

"I am a man of fixed and unbending principles, the first of which is to be flexible at all times."
— **Everett Dirksen**

Helicopters—My Addiction

In early February 2006, I attended an aviation trade show near Tacoma, Washington where I fell in love with helicopters.

When I was in high school, I remember seeing several of my friends learn to fly. I do recall some vague memories of jealousy, but I never imagined taking flight myself. It was far too much money, just not in my league. At least, that is where my belief system at the time kept me.

The private high school I attended actually had a small fixed wing flight program, and the cost of a private pilot rating at the time was about sixteen hundred dollars—a small fraction of what it is today, but far more than what I thought I could afford at the time because I was busy working to pay for my and my sister's tuition. With work, band, choir, and school, I soon forgot about the desire to fly.

Then the years went by. Marriage, chiropractic school, starting a new office on a thin shoestring, and supporting a growing family, along with not having any financial coaching to that point, quickly settled me into the mind-set of financial survival, a habit my wife today kindly reminds me I haven't quite shaken. Braces, private school tuition, not to mention my own sizable student loan repayment obligations kept my feet blissfully and literally on the ground.

Then in 1990, my younger sister Jeaneen gave me the gift of an introductory flight in a Cessna 150. I recall enjoying the flight, but somehow the potential reality of my becoming a pilot didn't sink in. Again several years went by, divorce, more financial struggle, and then one day, I decided I needed a hobby, an emotional and physical outlet. So I called the local flight school, scheduled a lesson, and started training. It was a great escape—a way to leave the struggles of raising kids, keeping a fledgling practice together, and all my other obligations. It became a way just to stay sane.

I'd like to say I attained my private rating in record time; however, life again intervened (of my own creation of course) and I moved through a succession of instructors, finally taking my airplane private rating exam in the summer of 2004.

I remember fondly the first time I really soloed. I headed out toward the foothills above Enumclaw and just enjoyed flying on my own for the first time. I felt like a hawk. The sun was shining, the mountain was as beautiful as ever and it was just me! No one else. I'll never forget that feeling of accomplishment and the soaring spiritual feeling it brought to me.

I couldn't get enough. I wanted to fly as much as possible. With money being fairly tight, I couldn't allow myself an "aerial fix" very often, but when I did, I enjoyed it. I flew off and on, putting together enough hours at the stick to stay safe and keep my interest (and myself) alive. Then early in the fall of 2004, I heard about the Kenmore seaplane base and drove up to the north end of Lake Washington to see what it was all about. After a brief tour and an explanation of the requirements for a seaplane rating, I signed up, and three days later, I took my floatplane check ride.

What a kick! I can't recommend it more highly (I can hear those un-enlightened spouses giving a collective groan). I was able to meet some great people at Kenmore, finding the service and professionalism at the base to be top notch. And I found out that just the year before, Harrison Ford, in preparation for his role in the film *Six Days, Seven Nights*, had been there falling in love with those floating airplanes himself. Of course he had to buy one, or two!

Not owning a floatplane is a particular disadvantage for those smitten with that particular species of flying bug. Due to insurance restrictions, floatplanes are typically not available for rental like regular fixed gear airplanes. So it was almost a year before I flew that beautiful yellow Super Cub again. And I haven't quite materialized my own amphibian, but I know it will happen when the timing is right. I can wait. Barely.

I flew regular fixed wing on and off for a couple of years, connecting with some new and old friends who either had a plane or were instructors, so I was able to sharpen my skills to a degree.

Then came that fateful winter day in February of 2006. I innocently walked into the Northwest Aviation Show, walked around a few of the aisles, turned a corner, and there she was! I somehow remember seeing something like a halo, maybe some soft harp music in the background, but however I recall it, there sat the most beautiful collection of gangly looking metal, plastic, and what-have-you that has ever graced the earth! A helicopter! And someone had painted it bright yellow to help snare unsuspecting, generally well-behaved family men like me!

Then to add the coup de grace, the young instructor invited me to climb inside. He looked to be all of about ten years old, but he could recognize a fellow lost soul. After a few brief words of instruction, he helped me up into the machine. I settled back into the seat and the universe suddenly made sense to me. I instantly knew I was made to fly helicopters! Okay, chiropractic is a worthy endeavor and I will probably be adjusting until the day I fly into the proverbial sunset, but this was serious! I knew that a hawk like me was not meant to scramble along the ground, trailing my wings (however figuratively) along in the dust.

It was all over—there was no going back. I scheduled a demo flight for April; then to give those around me a deceptively subtle conviction that I was still sane, I waited until June to start training. It went quickly from there. I'd like to say it didn't create an overwhelming financial strain. It did. Or that I wasn't distracted from other worthy pursuits. I was. I couldn't (okay, chose not to) help myself, and thankfully, my wife Melanie chose to adopt an accepting attitude and wait for me to come to my senses.

My private helicopter rating was passed that fall; then I moved on to my commercial rating the next spring. The next step was my instructor rating a year later. It all made sense. Really! With an instructor rating, you can have someone else pay for it and you get to fly and log the time! Okay, sure the student is typically some young kid unintentionally trying to end your life by screwing you into the ground, but hey, it's flying!

It would be a good conclusion to this chapter in my life to say that students were lined up around the block, and I flew happily into the sunset. Not quite.

The economy instead flew south, and along with it went most of the available student financing for budding helicopter drivers. Add to that the not so small detail that I had a growing chiropractic practice with employees to manage and patients to attend. Most of the available students went to the young guys, the ones who by necessity (and availability as well) were present on a daily basis to give the intro flights and nurture a group of students.

But I'm not complaining here. Flying helicopters is in my blood, and I can't see that changing while I have the physical capacity to accomplish it. That gives me quite a few years yet… and I am looking forward to wearing the paint off of many a set of rotor blades.

I have been asked many times by people sincerely wanting to know what it is about the machines that attracts me. "Is it like flying airplanes?" they ask. I typically answer by giving a comparison. Imagine if flying were like food; then airplanes are to helicopters what dry crackers are to a piece of moist chocolate cake.

Maybe the appeal to me is the difficulty. Recently, I had a last year chiropractic student named Phil visit Seattle for a few days. After he shadowed me in my office for a day or so, we had a chance to take a flight. It was a beautiful fall day, colors brilliant, the slight wind just right, the lowering angle of the sun setting off the fall foliage just perfectly. We flew toward the city, settled into a friend's backyard to do some brief business, then took off again for Seattle. A few careful circles around the Space Needle, an over-flight of the Seattle waterfront and skyline, and we headed back to the hangar. A great way to introduce a visitor to the sights of our lovely city.

About halfway through the flight, he turned to me and said over the intercom, "You really like things that are difficult, don't you?" Wow…he really nailed it right on the head. That is a very central reason why I love the heli so much. It takes one hundred percent concentration, both feet, both hands, and all your soul.

The flip side of that character trait, Chester being who he is, is that we can also make our relationships, whether they are with money, human beings, or time difficult. I have had a historical tendency to make things hard, a mistaken belief that for anything to be of value it must be difficult, even painful.

Hmmm…something to think about. A real eye-opener for me.

I thanked Phil for his insightful observation, however unintentionally brutal it was. We tend to agree with belief systems that sustain and support darling Chester. It's kind of like having an evil twin, someone whom at times you would really like to dismiss permanently. The problem is, like the old saying goes, "We have found the enemy and he is us."

For me it is flying helicopters. What is it for you? What are you not doing today because of some combination of fears and

"I can't"? If you were to roll out of bed tomorrow, and without letting Chester talk you out of it, went on to do for that day the very thing that lit you up and made you soar, what would it be?

It is not too late. Place your intention on discovering your passion. Pursue it with abandon. Life is to be enjoyed. In JOY!

7

OBSERVING CHESTER

"Always remember that you are unique, just like everyone else."
— **Allison Boulter**

Chester "unplugged"

Probably my first dramatic experience with observing a Chester-like fear-mind occurred when I was about ten years old.

Mr. Jones was my school friend Lisa's father. Today, I can see how he was apparently a tortured soul completely controlled by his fear and ego. The incident that sticks out in my memory happened one weekend when my parents were out of town and my older brother was left in charge. Probably sensing this was a recipe for disaster, my folks had arranged for the Jones family to pick us up and take us to church.

When the Joneses drove up that Saturday morning, it was obvious Mr. Jones was very angry for some reason and taking his wrath out on his poor wife. We all piled into their station wagon and headed off to church. We had only gone a few hundred yards down the road when his wife, who was driving, made the error of again offending Mr. Jones. He very abruptly reached over, turned the ignition of the car off and ordered her to let the car coast to a stop while all the time berating her mercilessly in front of not only his children, but my siblings and me as well. This was a foam-flecked tirade of verbal abuse. I must have been quite a picture myself, staring open-mouthed at this spectacle.

At that age, I had not accumulated a tremendous amount of experience, let alone understanding, of the extent of the fear-induced ego tantrum. I could not comprehend Mr. Jones' purpose for this display. I remember thinking he was probably insane, a diagnosis that was accurate, but not understood by either of us. What was interesting was that those around him (especially his family) excused, dismissed, and seemed to minimize his behavior. Or maybe they were simply afraid, perhaps less for their physical safety, than from fear this malady was somehow contagious.

In the earlier years of our marriage, my wife Melanie observed similar, but less dramatic behavior in my family—I would like to say that it involved someone other than myself; however, I must confess to the insanity. She would notice that due to my particular placement in the unspoken hierarchy of my own immediate family, my sometimes irrational behavior would be simply dismissed. My parents and siblings would choose not to see the misbehaving elephant in the room and accommodated the most disrespectful behavior.

Okay, enough about me; let's get back to Mr. Jones.

As I observed this gentleman and a few other "special" folks in our church family, I quickly learned that the church inexplicably excused and harbored these "special ones" in society. The world outside was the danger, while the tortured souls on the inside, the victims, did what they had to do to rationalize most any behavior and survive this wretched earth in the hopes of heaven someday. Harbored within the walls of the church, "sin" could be kept at bay and made a scapegoat for the fear-mind's shenanigans. Looking back, I realize that personal accountability, on any kind of spiritually responsible level, was a foreign concept.

Mr. Jones was the audio man at our church. He marched dramatically up and down the aisles, plugging and unplugging microphones, often in the middle of a musical presentation or sermon. Any problem was an opportunity for a highly entertaining display. His lightning quick emphatic step and gestures were a familiar sight in our church. He closely guarded the PA booth in the back of the sanctuary, a pew only shared with the lucky few who passed his close inspection.

I remember feeling sorry for my friend, Lisa, her sisters, and especially her mother. I often wondered what it was like inside their house, and later, I learned there were some serious dysfunctional issues occurring under that roof over the years.

With the passage of time, I realized Mr. Jones was struggling mightily with his own Chester. He had spent years in reaction, not understanding what was happening, not realizing that he had given his fear-mind full control. Feeding on fear, drama, and anger, his fear-mind was rarely tempered by the quietness of consciousness. I learned much from observing Mr. Jones' struggle with his Chester and how painful and embarrassing this fear reaction can be, even though at the time I did not understand the concept. I saw the destruction such acting out was creating in his own family. But probably most importantly, I saw what I did not want to become, and what frightened me was that I saw myself as powerless to prevent it.

If the fear-mind is allowed to define you, it will convince you that your fear-identified self is your only hope for survival. The good news is you can reclaim your identity and refuse to allow the fear-mind to dictate the definition of your personality.

With this understanding, empathy follows. As the years passed, I could see the Joneses' lives mellowing. Each year saw a decrease in the intensity of the dramatic display. Either Mr. Jones was getting tired or he was learning. I think both. To this day we get a very nice Christmas card from them. What impresses me is the extreme level of patience and understanding

Mrs. Jones has shown to live with her husband all these years. I have also come to realize that Mrs. Jones was also the co-creator and benefactor of this experience. This was her opportunity to grow and learn as well.

Because life's purpose is for us to understand and spiritually evolve, we bring into our lives whatever lessons are needed to accomplish this goal. Some of these lessons will by necessity be very painful. Chester's grip can only be loosened by observing his insanity. But first, our attention must be gained.

You are capable of rising beyond the tyranny of a fear-infused mind. Opportunities to raise your consciousness above the level of fear surround you. You cannot help but attract them. You will either resist or invite in the lesson. And it is best not to judge the opportunity as it presents itself. Lessons take us out of our comfort zone, so expect to feel uncomfortable.

Reclaiming your consciousness takes nothing more than observing Chester and his fear. Once this happens, you regain your power and Chester and his forceful activity are neutralized.

The pivotal point, the window of opportunity, is the moment of choice. When we truly see, in the absence of fear, the damage done by our fear-mind, we can choose an alternative.

Dare to be uncomfortable. Be bold enough to bring Chester into the light of accountability. Call his bluff. Quietly observe his immature nature. He won't forgive you for it, but he has no power over you when in the light of observation, you hold him accountable.

Avoiding Action Motivated by Fear

I made a promise to myself several months ago (and actually have renewed the promise thousands of times since) not to make any more decisions based on or motivated by fear. Each time, Chester has smugly chuckled from his corner, "Good luck with that, buddy," to let me know I was on my own with this resolution.

Action motivated by fear can only create more drama and conflict. Action motivated by awareness and observation engages and recruits the cooperation of Source. Coincidence and serendipity are the natural consequences rather than the crazy pain scenarios of Chester's world.

An example of action motivated by fear was my first marriage. I married early. Really early. I was barely nineteen when I first walked down the wedding aisle. Convinced that life was better in the adult world, I was eager to move forward, be a man, and most of all, show my family and friends I was now "grown up." The problem is I was thinking about and reacting more to them than thinking about myself. I wasn't being selfish enough—an incredibly foreign concept to me at that time.

I can remember being in a hurry to get married. I wanted to experience the joys of marriage, have kids, and get some serious living done before the heavens opened up and Jesus came back to blow the whistle. "Okay, everybody, out of the pool!"

Not understanding relationships very well, I was swept along with the tide of hormones, emotions, and the sincere desire to be the "Big Man." Looking back on this time in my life, I have often wondered whether the rest of my family were as clueless as me. However, if at the time any of my family tried to talk some sense into me, I don't remember hearing it. I was on a mission and life was exciting, so let's get on with it already!

But as the wedding day drew near, I grew more nervous. That little voice was murmuring, then speaking a little louder, then screaming at me, "Wake the hell up!" I can imagine the little voice trumpeting as my collision course with the "I do" came closer.

When I tried to talk to my fiancée about my concerns, doubts, and fears, she was less than receptive. She had her own plans, and slowing down definitely did not fit into them. In fact, because of the rough time in her own household, she declared that if we didn't get married, she would hurt herself, maybe even kill herself.

Not being emotionally mature or strong enough myself, I backed away from my convictions. I couldn't let someone in that much pain hurt herself because of me. So I folded. The marriage plans continued.

I had made a very big decision based on fear. Fear that we would be embarrassed in front of our friends and family. Fear that my fiancée would be hurt. Fear that I would be considered immature—never mind that I was.

So this was the road I traveled. Married at nineteen with no understanding of the healthy path to a satisfactory relationship. We were both making it up as we went along. And I know we were not alone in this. How many young married couples have any shred of a clue about what they are getting into?

Those early years were very hard. We moved from Idaho immediately after we got married. Working at four dollars an hour as an apprentice cabinet-maker just didn't go far in supporting a household, no matter how small the house. My childhood friend, Bruce, back in Washington State, offered me a job with plenty of work at ten dollars an hour. Feeling I could not pass up such an offer, we moved to Seattle. This was not well received by my new bride, but we felt it was what we had to do.

Looking back, I am surprised our marriage survived as long as it did. But thankfully, young kids are resilient and a bit naive, the latter probably being the most helpful in such situations. As the years went by, we became very familiar with the interstate between Seattle and Boise. We drove that road in all kinds of weather. I quickly became an expert in driving on snowy mountain passes. True, we had a few mishaps, slid off the road a few times, but thankfully, no one was hurt, just a few repairs needed on the fenders.

This fear-based decision to marry so young steered us onto a rocky path for many years, but even this detour was still on the road to understanding. I am convinced now that no decision made is ever really a mistake, just that some lessons are more painful than others. Of course we had many good times as well, and we have four beautiful and strong sons from that marriage, an incredible blessing to us both, and I am sure, to the rest of our extended families as well.

One of the major lessons I gleaned from my first marriage is to be more watchful about how and why I make decisions. I now realize much of this wisdom comes with time and is largely due to trial and error. And now as I observe myself in the decision-making process, I can clearly see the impact of Chester and his language of fear. It is easier to see the potential impact of the fear-based option versus the centered non-fear choice.

And with this maturity and awareness, you see that a choice is indeed truly a choice. As I have observed Chester over the years, I am really starting to appreciate that choice is truly only a choice when we are aware enough to see what the fear-mind is capable of making us do.

Choice in the absence of understanding is actually not a choice. At best, what we see as choice is a conditioned response actuated by fear. The result will most likely lead to a very challenging learning experience, likely accompanied by a healthy measure of pain.

But the wonderful thing about pain is that it will eventually lead us back to our lesson. The variable is, how much suffering are we willing to endure? How long do we want to delay the lesson that life is so willing to provide?

From my observation of the world, I think some of us must be really stubborn! We are thickheaded to the point of solidity. Sometimes, this planet seems to be one seething cauldron of insanity and suffering. Then from a different perspective, it is viewed as a sphere of beauty filled with conscious souls all on their own unique and relentless path to consciousness. As I step further away from the interference of Chester in my observation, I prefer the latter.

It took me years to realize that pain is not the punishment of Satan due to my transgressions. Nor is it the justice of the universe. It is simply the smoke of resistance pluming upward from the reactivity generated by Chester. I can picture him as a stubborn mule being dragged down the road to enlightenment— all four hooves firmly planted in resistance, sparks and sod flying! Interesting how viewing Chester as an ass really fits!

Your challenge is to take a look at how you make decisions. Can you quietly and honestly say to yourself that a decision is being made without the motivation of fear? Begin this discovery by taking advantage of this small window of clarity and looking at the process of your decision-making. Observe how you feel during the process and then look at the result. What are you learning about how you are making decisions?

"A man of genius makes no mistakes.
His errors are volitional and are the portals of discovery."
— James Joyce

The genius that James Joyce is referring to here is the innate genius of Spirit. How exciting to know that each conscious decision is an invitation to new and intentional discovery!

"Right now you are one choice away from a new beginning."
— Oprah Winfrey

When we understand our "errors" really aren't mistakes, we will arrive at the truly liberating discovery that there is no judgment hanging over us in our decision-making. I know that this flies in the face of much of our conventional wisdom, especially the "divine" wisdom shared by most religions.

"A person who never made a mistake never tried anything new."
— Albert Einstein

Error and sin are usually pretty well spelled out. According to the church, you choose at your peril, maybe even your eternal peril. All of your actions are viewed, monitored and written down somewhere for eventual judgment. Just like Santa Claus, "He" knows when you've been "bad." This sounds like an environment of fear to me.

Now you may think I am being a little too harsh on my church friends. If this is the case, please forgive me. This is not my intention. I was raised in the church, and I will forever appreciate the many positive results of that experience. My purpose is to shed a little light on the opportunities that give us a chance to modify our behavior and not make decisions in fear. Are you able objectively to take a look at your church and belief systems and determine whether this is the case? Are you structuring your life in response to fear or freedom?

The movie *Braveheart* comes to mind whenever I hear or utter the word "freedom." William Wallace went to his death with this word on his lips and the concept of freedom burned into his soul. Here was a man who refused to live his life in fear. He could have walked away and succumbed to authority, yet he chose to live his own life. This very dramatic portrayal is not just locked away in the confines of history. We play out different versions of this scenario numerous times every day of our lives. With increased awareness, we will see more opportunities to choose to live our lives with joyful intention, without fear.

Recognizing Control of the Fear-Mind

It is usually quite easy to recognize a person controlled by his or her fear-mind. The attributes of Chester, such as anxiety, suspicion, anger, etc. are usually the first responses in such a person.

How do you know when you have given control to and identified with Chester? When you see yourself thinking and acting in the realm of the duality and opposites. Happiness and sorrow, politeness and anger, love and hate. These expressions of the fear-mind are typically motivated by external factors. "She made me mad" or "He makes me so happy…."

True love, joy, and acceptance are qualities and concepts unfortunately beyond the understanding of the "opposite mind." Authentic love and joy have no opposites as they arise without cause from the Source mind. The fear-mind cannot know them or even grasp a rudimentary knowledge of them. In fact, Chester and the fear-mind will vanish in their presence. So Chester is mortally afraid of being in the presence of loving observation.

Consequently, Chester will necessarily do whatever it takes to pull you away from the centered position of observing. Do you need a little drama in your life? Chester can help with that. In the guise of protecting you, he will manufacture a threat and initiate his idea of an appropriate response. Of course, these are all Chester's self-serving efforts at self-preservation.

The incredible opportunity is to recognize the process and short circuit Chester's plans. As Barney Fife, my favorite character from *The Andy Griffith Show*, would say, "Nip it! Nip it in the bud!"

Speaking of dear Barney, he reminds me a lot of Chester. So eager to please, but oblivious to his craziness.

In one episode of *The Andy Griffith Show*, Barney and Andy are preparing for a performance with the local choir. The scene opens with the choir happily singing away, enjoying the harmony and togetherness the activity brings. Then Barney joins in. It is soon apparent there is a bad seed in the crowd. Someone is singing terribly off tune. Furtive looks by people in the choir and straining ears somehow fail to ferret out the culprit. But of course, this is *The Andy Griffith Show*; these people would be too polite, and therefore hesitant, to confront their good friend.

Finally, Barney, true to his eagerness to be helpful, has a word with the choir director. He selflessly offers quietly to move around through the group and find the offending voice. Amazingly, he fails to find the off-color singer. Barney is truly perplexed; he was so sure that his stellar sleuthing skills would be successful. They resume singing, the problem still with them.

Meanwhile, Andy and the director have realized Barney is the one with the voice of a very ill hyena. They are perplexed about how to remedy the situation without hurting Barney's feelings until Andy comes up with a beautiful plan.

They will offer Barney the chance to sing a solo! Now it is not difficult at all to convince Barney to do the special part in the song. He, like our friend Chester, is a bit of a blow-hard, his ego very dependent on how others view him. But as he begins to bellow out the solo part, the director and Andy inform Barney that because his voice is "so good, so powerful" he must tone it down a bit so as not to overshadow the rest of the chorale with his magnificent tenor. In fact, they ask him to sing into the microphone so softly that, you guessed it, they manage to fade him completely into the background. They go on to perform the song and everyone is happy.

This story portrays wonderfully the fragile state of Chester's ego. He is eternally convinced that the source of disharmony is outside of himself. Disharmony in our internal environment, just like in the choir, is always someone else's fault! It is Chester's job to bring the offender to light and if necessary to harsh justice!

By observing Chester, we can learn ways to placate his voice in our heads without letting him overpower us.

8

LEAVING FEAR BEHIND

"I am a man, and I can change, if I have to, I guess...."
— **The Red Green Show**

The Red Green Show is a hilarious (and some females would say scary) look into the interesting world of male behavior. This is the show that promotes duct tape as the ultimate fix-all. At the end of each half hour show, all the men get together for their lodge meeting and recite the man's creed, "I am a man and I can change, if I have to, I guess…"

I would say, without a doubt, that change is the most challenging opportunity for growth we ever experience, particularly change that requires accepting and then leaving behind those belief systems that keep us mired in our continuous cycle of self-created fear.

Chester will vigorously defend the wisdom of "not rocking the boat" with his mentality of, "Who needs change? Hey, it's not so bad! Who do you think you are?" Resistance to change is fundamental to the ego consciousness. Your ego or fear-mind, represented by dear Chester, will create with laser-sharp intention, the patterns that sustain his current existence and supporting belief systems.

Your opportunity, when presented with a window of consciousness (or awareness), is to break the pattern. Your Source mind, with discipline and a new target of intention, can create into "reality" your wildest dreams.

But when you take the opportunity to change, the people in your support circle will be threatened if they are identified with the fear-mind. The friends, family, and co-workers you have attracted to date will be agitated and uncomfortable in the presence of your newfound awareness.

Your opportunity will be to create a new team, although this will not necessarily require new (or different) people. Knowing most of your friends are creating their own paths of spiritual awakening, you will likely see change in your circle as well. Remember, change is just as hard for them—even harder if they lack understanding of your reason for change. But with your example, they will also have the opportunity to create a window of conscious awareness for themselves. As this occurs, be patient and allowing toward them and yourself. Allow them to have the experiences they have created, AND allow yourself the ability to re-create your life according to your Source's intention and direction.

Expect and prepare yourself for the new. If the people on your support team truly support the authentic you, they will come around, maybe not right away, but be assured when they do, it will be at the perfect time for them.

During the dark years following my divorce, a well-meaning friend told me my disappearing friends would come around, that they would eventually forgive. I wasn't so sure, but there would eventually be a few exceptions to the general pattern of judgment.

Several years after my divorce, a woman who had been my friend since we were both in the sixth grade, approached me to ask my forgiveness for her part in the shunning and antipathy following my divorce. Years earlier, after chiropractic school as my wife and I were settling into our new life, she and my wife became good friends. Unfortunately, with the divorce, she felt she needed to support the drama created by my estranged wife. She felt she had to choose the "right" and separate herself from the "wrong".

Her request for forgiveness touched me. She acknowledged her part in the drama of our separation and eventually observed the fault-finding activity of her fear-mind. But it took several years for this to happen.

The difficult part of acceptance is that other people's perfect timing may not be in your lifetime, or even theirs! Some people have created this life experience to be a sort of "spiritual vacation." Maybe they don't want or intend to do much in the way of personal spiritual development this time around. It is not for us to judge, push, or expect what they will or will not accomplish.

In *Power vs. Force*, David Hawkins indicates it is very unlikely for the vast majority of people to make a significant consciousness change in their lifetimes. Quantum leaps in awareness are rare, and they are to be celebrated when they occur!

The way of peace is to be thankful for the friendship, love, and support received in this moment. That is the Magic of allowing and acceptance. When we understand the ongoing dynamic of this physical experience, we can have a much greater appreciation for the gift of those who share our lives. They each truly have their own unique life's work and purpose, and you have yours. Celebrate the gift and magic of the coincidence of sharing this space and time with them. Coincidence, that arranging by the universe of matching the right person and/ or opportunity with you in this moment, is special. It is truly Magic!

The divine wonder of being in this moment with another vibrant soul is priceless. When we attempt to change them, we potentially break this beautiful moment's fragile bond of synchronicity.

Living "out there" is painful. When we perceive that our joy is dependent on the "rightness" of our external environment, we set ourselves up for disappointment. The futility of attempting to change what is outside of us invariably leads to frustration and more pain. Remain centered in self. Accept that this form of "selfishness" is the catalyst for true and lasting change on a personal as well as global scale.

Live by example this path of joy. Living by force, expecting others to be different to make things better, is living outside of our Self. It is pain. Allow, love, forgive, and accept. Be the change the world needs. The challenge is that Chester does not speak this language. He squirms on his stool in the corner when you resonate and vibrate acceptance, forgiveness, and allowing. "But someone will hurt us, take advantage of us—WE MUST DEFEND!" is his warning.

Joy vs. Happiness

Happiness is fleeting by definition. It is a result of external factors where joy is un-caused. Joy is an essential part of our spirit. Joy has no opposite, so it is always with you and independent of the "good or bad" of any given situation.

People tend to rely on the addiction of happiness. Happiness leaves the perfection of the present moment and anticipates salvation in the future. "If I get this, then I'll be happy." "If I find the 'right' person for my mate, I will live happily ever after." Such thoughts are illusion and a setup for the back and forth seesaw duality of the pain and sorrow dynamic.

You can learn to observe and thereby accept the happiness and sorrow Chester serves on his platter of offerings. Feel them, but don't let them draw you back into identification with your ego fear-mind. The back and forth can get very tiring. With practice and observation, you can stay centered in your joy source and be unmoved by the tidal fluctuations of externally caused emotions such as sorrow and happiness.

Most married people can remember the "up and down" craziness of the marriage's first year. Still very caught up in the unrealistic, hormone-infused drama, most couples find the ego mind's antics exhausting. One minute you are making your mate "happy." The next minute you are the spawn of Satan. Since your worthiness is measured by what "you can do for me," your usefulness varies from moment to moment. And this goes for the guys too!

I can't tell you how many times I have heard male friends say, "I can't figure it out! She's a bitch one minute, then everything is fine." If happiness is motivated by fear, the result is an inevitable slide into pain and sorrow. You just have to add a little time.

The answer is joy, but first a little awareness of what is true joy can be very helpful.

As mentioned earlier, joy is without cause. It just "is." It does not depend on whether supper is on the table or your mother-in law is dining with you. It remains constant when the checkbook's balance does not. Joy is the background observation of the craziness of life, not the result of whether the day is going my way.

This concept was difficult for me. I remember sitting on the island of Molokai during my vision quest, trying to wrap my mind around it. Of course at that time, I didn't realize joy was a concept my thinking mind (primarily Chester) couldn't begin to comprehend. How could you have joy if everything wasn't "good"? Do you mean joy could be present at a funeral or when a family member is sick?

That was the tough one to understand. Joy is not caused or diminished by circumstance. Joy is the thread of spiritual presence that infuses all of our experience. It just is there as the very essence of who we really are.

Joy is not a feeling to experience someday in some far off heaven. It is here today. Neither is it a reward for some future attainment of worthiness. We are worthy now.

The main reason religion doesn't work for me anymore is because I have come to realize that you and I already are worthy and that "heaven" is now, so what then can any church give me or you?

Nothing. No thing.

That realization was really hard for me to accept. I had invested so many years in my church, and I knew so many wonderful people still very intent on maintaining those long held belief systems and codes of conduct.

Every few months I get talked into attending a special function at my old church, the same church that "dis-membered" me, and that my parents still attend. I feel the old feelings of warmth and belonging rise up, and the temptation to step back into the embrace of the congregation is very strong.

Very strong that is until someone opens his or her mouth and speaks the belief systems. Then the fear-based, rigid limits of the dogma shines through—the fear-laced adherence to what is "right" and the avoidance of what the fear-mind labels as "wrong." Then I realize there truly is no going back. Once you step away from identifying with Chester, you have moved to another place. Your light of understanding has transmuted the dark shadows of ignorance, so you cannot put the proverbial genie back in the bottle.

So I am learning to allow and let be. I am learning to be thankful for the friends, the love, and the caring. And additionally, I have learned to guard myself more. Now I am a little more careful about how far I emotionally extend myself, particularly at the invitation of the fear-mind. It is easier to stay centered when I step back and observe the old feelings and where they led.

Step back and observe. Keep an eye on Chester and his big mouth.

"Silence is the true friend that never betrays."
— **Confucius**

How can we know we have what it takes to leave our fear behind and create a new world for our Self?

You will attract and manifest, by nature, all of the tools and people for your support team you will ever need. Jesus taught us to look at the beauty of the simple flower. Its glory is complete. Anything added to the simple architecture would destroy the beauty, not increase it. Our authentic selves are like the flower, complete, and therefore, perfect.

Eckhart Tolle tells the story of passing on the roadside a beggar sitting on a box. The destitute person was there day after day, sitting alone, begging for assistance. He was asking for the abundance he could not feel, see, or expect. When asked what was in the box he was sitting on, the beggar said, "Nothing; it's just an old box." When the man was asked to look inside, to his amazement he found the box was filled with gold. His abundance had been with him all along! He had been sitting on it, ignorant of the treasure that was already his!

I agree with Tolle. I have nothing to give you other than my experience in looking inside. You are invited to take a look inside and set aside the layers of disbelief and fear.

My childhood experience of God and Church convinced me that my abundance, physical and spiritual, was conditional and "out there." It was just beyond reach, but attainable if I worked hard enough or pleased the right people. I always seemed to come up short, but not from lack of trying. My belief system said that someday, when I was complete, good enough, loved enough, some One or some God, would give to me my "pot of gold."

I invite you to realize who you are and what you have. This realization will allow you to see the person you have always been. The You has not changed, been lost, misplaced, or damaged. The you whom you think you are, whom Chester tells you that you are, is an illusion, a counterfeit of your essential Self.

You have the power to leave fear behind. This power is nowhere else. It is within your nature.

Once realized, this new awareness will allow you to see the person you have been all along. So in truth, change is nothing more than a new understanding of self. There is no physical change. There truly is no place to go! No heaven to find. You don't need to pay some guru thousands of dollars to give you anything you don't already have. Our work is the shedding of our B.S. (belief systems). There is no thing to acquire except how to know and tame Chester and his self-talk. Our fear-mind or ego grasps tight. Source lets go and allows (Let go and let God).

Chester, bless his heart (three sizes too small), loves shiny objects. One of my favorite boyhood stories was *Where the Red Fern Grows* by Wilson Rawls. This classic story tells of a young boy with limited means obsessed with acquiring two hunting dogs. Much of the story is about his journey toward realizing his dream; however, there is a later experience in the book that perfectly illustrates my point about the fear-mind and the difficulty of letting go.

After the boy gets his dogs, he is eager to begin hunting, specifically for raccoons. But before he can do so, he needs to train his dogs, and to train them, he needs a raccoon pelt so the dogs can develop their scent and tracking skills. The conundrum is he needs trained dogs to get a raccoon and a raccoon to train his dogs. What to do?

Then Grandpa comes to the rescue. They head off into the forest river bottom with a handful of nails, a hammer, a drill brace, and a small piece of shiny tin cut from a food can. Finding a log by the river, the grandfather drills a hole into the log. Then he hammers some nails at an angle into the log so the nails' points enter the hole several inches down. Dropping a piece of bright tin into the hole, the trap is complete. "But how will that trap my raccoon, Grandpa?" The boy is sure Grandpa is once again pulling his leg, something that has always given his grandfather great pleasure.

The grandfather explains that although raccoons are smart and crafty, they have an insatiable curiosity. They cannot resist a bright piece of metal. The raccoon will reach in, grasp the shining treasure tight, and then become trapped because he will not let go even when approached by the hunting dogs.

So it is with the fear-mind. Chester equates spiritual change and conscious awakening with his literal death. He will not let go of fear-based belief systems—even if it means bringing tremendous suffering into your life. Letting go seems so simple, yet most of us cannot let go. Letting go is the opportunity to step through the window of spiritual transformation and allow change. This window is created by awakening of Spirit and is perceived as a direct threat by Chester.

Chester is comfortable with his position and the status quo. Although very unconscious in a spiritual sense, the status quo is familiar and safe. If Chester perceives change coming and a threat to his well-maintained identity with fear, he will resist—with savage resistance.

How to let go? Just open your hand. It's that simple. Not easy, but simple. You have at your disposal a consciousness that the raccoon does not possess. Drop the once attractive object or belief. Open your heart and mind to the you that is You! The real you. Not that shabby image of you that Chester treasures in his corner of fear.

My early childhood education was supplemented by watching *Sesame Street*. Some of the characters, Bert and Ernie in particular, were pretty insightful. Anyone who watched the show remembers Ernie's affection for his rubber duckie. In one episode, Bert and Ernie give an important lesson when they sing, "You gotta put down the duckie, put down the duckie, put down the duckie if you want to play the saxophone!" Definitely a classic.

Like Ernie or the raccoon, we find it really tough to drop things we cherish—even potentially destructive belief patterns. They become a part of our identity, consciousness, and behavior. We have survived so long relying on the ego that the alternative is incomprehensible.

Even though the answer, "Just drop it" is simple, it is definitely easier said than done.

Ernie thankfully figured it out. He got to play his song. But he had to let go; he had to drop the duckie first to make it happen.

We can struggle an entire lifetime defending our right to hang on to fear. In its many forms, be it anger, righteousness, or patriotic fervor, fear will prevent us from singing or playing our unique and precious life-song.

And our purpose in life is to SING OUR SONG! If we exit this beautiful expression of life with our song unsung, the world is much the poorer for it.

Like the raccoon in *Where the Red Fern Grows*, we have a choice. We can open our consciousness and drop the fear IF we have the understanding of how our fear, and more specifically, our Chester can cloud our ability to choose.

Most of the work in this process is recognizing that we do indeed have an irrational grip on a belief system that does not serve our higher spiritual purpose. When we are aware enough to recognize the destructive effect of Chester's control, just the power of our observation will give us the room to loosen that grip and set us free.

Your work is to recognize, observe, and send Chester back to his stool in the corner. When we are in the present moment, Chester has no power. His inflammatory suggestions are recognized for the craziness they are. Where earlier we were ready to jump into battle, now we see that the image of the threat is but an illusion painted on the screen of our fear-based mind.

"Your key to change…is to let go of fear."
— Roseanne Cash

Opening our Window of Awareness

"The mind is like a parachute, it works best when open."
— Unknown

I love to fly. Okay, most flying. My friend John has a biplane built specifically for aerobatics. He loves to fly upside down, in loops, crazy orientations that strain the g-force meter on the panel far past my comfort zone.

He invited me to go flying a few months ago, and being the aviation nut I am, I jumped at the chance. Even recalling my less than fond memories of spin training in my small plane classes, any excuse to soar into the blue sky is gratefully accepted.

I must admit, when he rolled the hangar door open and I first saw his multi-colored bi-plane, I shared his excitement! Its rainbow of colors sparkled in the sunlight! "Strap this on," he said handing me a parachute. "You won't need it, but just in case…" Talk about a confidence builder!

After a pre-flight and some instruction on how to exit the plane in an emergency, we soared off into the blue sky and spent the next hour hanging upside down, seeing how far we could spin the g-meter.

We returned to earth uneventfully, but it took me until the better part of the next day for my stomach to join me back on the ground. But it was thrilling! I was thankful for not having to open my chute. Straight and level flying for me, thank you!

Just like the old saying about parachutes, the mind works best when open to change. An "arms across the chest" refusal to experience the shedding of spiritually destructive belief systems will keep you enslaved to Chester's picture of comfort and safety.

The discouraging thing is to start each day on the repetitive merry-go-round of Chester's choosing.

"Keep walking, though there is no place to get to. Don't try to see through the distances. That is not for human beings. Move within, but do not move the way that fear makes you move."
— **Rumi**

What can you do to assist a change? Modify your life.

Dr. Mark Rademacher is a practice coach in Wisconsin who helped me to see how to create change and pull myself out of fear-based behavior.

His technique called for the use of "modifiers." Dr. R separated these modifiers into three classes: mild, moderate, and severe.

An example of mild modifiers would be taking a different route to work in the morning or listening to a different type of music. Other examples might be parking in a different parking spot at the office or re-arranging the furniture. These simple techniques don't seem very impressive; however, they work to upset Chester's world. It doesn't take much, but the results can be impressive.

A moderate modifier might be something a little more aggressive such as replacing a team member at work—something your fear has been avoiding—or attending that week long seminar on time-management that you keep putting off. These options take more risk and effort than the mild modifiers and are typically recommended when the situation calls for more aggressive action.

Severe modifiers are typically not recommended. These might include quitting your job, getting a divorce, moving to a different state, or choosing a new occupation. These really drive Chester insane! They also come with their own challenges and require commitment and spiritual presence.

Change in your life may not require a severe modifier. Chester can be unsettled and put on notice by a course of action that is relatively mild. It may be as simple as wearing a different shirt on Tuesdays!

Remember the movie *As Good As It Gets*? In this film, Jack Nicholson played a disturbed and obsessive gentleman who incorporates very profound techniques of obsessive-compulsive behavior to protect his fear-mind identity. Similarly, when Chester is allowed that level of control, he preserves his dominance with some really crazy behavior! In the movie, Nicholson's character was required to make some really scary changes in his life in order to arrive at his goal, namely a relationship with Helen Hunt's character.

How deeply entrenched is your fear-mind? How threatened would your Chester be if you made a few changes in your life?

Chester requires a high level of control to maintain his grip on your life. To do this he will perpetuate and control your environment and the content of your day and experience. Are you becoming aware of what your fear-mind is doing? What are you feeding your mind? What level of consciousness decides the television shows you watch, the movies you see and the books you read? Do you begin each day with intention in regard to what your mind absorbs, or are you a slave to Chester's default mode of approaching the day?

We are not the victims of our environment to the degree that many of us would believe. Unless of course our input selector switch is in the default position—the fear default.

Without intention, Chester will interpret every input as either a threat or an opportunity to support his agenda of fear-based response. Conscious intention sets Chester's agenda aside and puts your authentic self back in the driver's seat.

How do you accomplish this? It's actually quite easy as long as you remember your intention. However, if you get caught up again in the drama, default creation will again take over.

So, number one, awaken to the day with purpose, intention, and attention. Make a decision about how your day will go and proceed with that intent and expectation. When you feel emotions generated by fear, such as anger, entitlement, or anxiety, stop and center yourself. Picture Chester over in his corner creating the ruckus. Calm him with your observation and attention. Move through and beyond the drama.

You will be surprised at how easy and effective this technique is. The challenge is staying with it. In the beginning of your practice of presence, your attention will be challenged incessantly. But stay with it; it will get easier, more practiced, and eventually become automatic.

What Chester is counting on is your attention span. Ever notice the attention span of the average kindergartner? Ever wonder why most television and advertising is geared toward this age group? Chester is hoping you will tire and become distracted because with that small space of distraction comes his opportunity to reinstate fear, tension, and drama. But that's okay; as you experience his deception, you will become increasingly aware of each derailment and quickly bc able to bring yourself right back on track.

Practice. Practice. Practice. It's not hard; you are just in it for the long haul.

As you become more adept at presence, you will have the advantage over Chester simply due to your mature, non-fear level of attention. Believe me it's there. It's just rusty and crippled with disuse. Practice quiet observation wherever you find yourself—whether it's watching Chester and his reactions while driving in crazy traffic, dinner with your mother-in law, or simply riding the city bus. Develop your ability to watch calmly and not react. You will find this immensely empowering.

"The road to success is lined with many tempting parking spaces."
— Author Unknown

Chester is hoping you will be distracted and worn out by the constant work of observation. Stay the course. The goal is well worth the perseverance.

Learning about My Power of Creation

"Be careful what you wish for; you just might get it!"
— Author Unknown

I have never spent much time worrying about the passage of time. I have always felt and acted young, and the accumulating years haven't bothered me, much.

Until lately.

Next year, I turn fifty. My wife thinks this is hilarious. She has been waiting for me to catch up with her for a long time. She is a couple of years older than me and her sage advice regarding my advancing years is much appreciated. My pathetic pleadings to have a "mid-life crisis" have largely fallen on her deaf ears. No sympathy there.

I guess the biggest thing for me regarding turning fifty is the typical question: "What have I accomplished?" True, I've raised four boys and helped raise three girls. My chiropractic practice is considered successful, and I have felt very thankful for the privilege of sharing chiropractic with thousands of people. But making an impact in the business world has largely eluded me.

So recently, I began asking the universe for an education in business, or more specifically a mentor, someone who had been successful in a big way and was willing to teach me. My boys were getting older and my goal was to instruct them in the nuts of bolts of business as well as provide for them an opportunity to get some hands-on experience in business endeavors of their own.

I set about waiting very patiently for my lesson in business to arrive. Okay, maybe not very patiently….

Then my wife went to visit her family in Montana, leaving me unattended at home. She usually gets very nervous when she leaves, not so much from missing me, but from thinking, "Oh my God, I've left him at home again with the checkbook." I typically behave myself when it comes to money, but the occasional indiscretion tends to be associated with figures with lots of zeroes in them.

This time it wasn't so bad. While wandering through the empty house, I stumbled upon the couch in our downstairs media room. This room is typically considered "teenage land"

and best not entered by adults with any desire to retain their sanity. Throwing caution to the wind, I stepped inside and immediately confronted a crisis—a couch I had inherited from my younger brother during one of his moves. It was a very comfortable couch and had been much loved over the years, particularly by the youngsters in our household. But fifteen plus years of indoor gymnastics and the onslaught of teenage bodies had reduced it to a barely recognizable collection of tattered fabric and bits of foam.

It was time to clean house. On the spur of the moment, I backed my trusty pickup truck up to the house and wrestled the sofa into the back. A few extra bags of trash and yard waste completed the load and made me feel better about paying the minimum dump fee.

It felt good! Out with the old and in with the…well, this is where I get into trouble. The new. The empty spot in the downstairs den, even when all the dust bunnies and spider mummies were vacuumed up, left a big hole. A "friend" had gone to his reward and I felt the need to fill the gap.

Digging around in the recycling bin, I managed to recover the previous week's community newspaper. A brief scan down the "For Sale" column quickly brought me to the ad: "Leather (red) sectional for sale." And it was only a few miles away in the next town! I jumped back into my truck and drove over to check it out.

The color red probably wasn't my first pick, and fortunately, my wife was safely five hundred miles away. I did the perfunctory tape measuring ritual, even driving back home to measure the room. Bottom line, the sofa fit in the back of my truck (barely), and after negotiating the price, I set off for home to reassemble the new addition.

But the important part of this story is that Marilyn, who sold me the couch, and I turned out to have many mutual friends, so we spent quite a bit of time sharing stories and connecting the dots. After I mentioned chiropractic and aviation experience, Marilyn said I had to meet a business associate of hers, Jackson Tse. She was sure our shared interest in health care, flying, and things with motors in them was bound to initiate some mutual business venture. Her intuition proved solid.

A week later, I had the privilege to meet Jackson, and soon after, I was invited by Marilyn to celebrate Jackson's birthday with a few friends at the indoor cart track. His love for cars and his participation with the local Ferrari owners association pretty much assured that the surprise event would be a success.

My wife and two youngest boys joined me at the indoor cart track where we had a great time! Marilyn diplomatically suggested that since it was Jackson's birthday, I should make sure he won the race. I didn't do so well with Marilyn's suggestion— once I'm behind the wheel of a vehicle with a motor, any resemblance to calm thinking and sanity vanish quickly. My competitive instincts flared, the race became a blur and the time passed far too fast....No, I didn't win. Marilyn's college-age daughter took the checkered flag. Must have been some oil on the track—yes, that was it....

While waiting for our results to be posted, Jackson and I had a chance to chat a bit and get to know each other. We talked about airplanes, his degree in aeronautical engineering, and his love for cars. Toward the end of our discussion, I suggested he should do some aviation projects. He thought about it for a few seconds, then said, "Sounds like a good idea; you can be our aviation director!"

I didn't really think he was anywhere close to serious since we had just met. But when I later mentioned it to Marilyn, she replied, "Jackson never says anything like that unless he means it."

A couple of weeks later, my name and short bio were on the management team page of his corporate Web site and I had received new business cards with the title "Aviation Director." I was a bit surprised but also honored. Okay, now what?

Since then, life has been pretty much a blur. Not only have I had the privilege to learn from a serious business mentor, but I have been none too gently shoved into the pool's deep end. This technique is not for the timid and faint of heart, but nevertheless, quite effective.

Jackson has been a significant principal in the development of businesses that have sold for hundreds of millions of dollars. He is greatly respected, domestically and internationally, by giants in the business world. I could not have paid enough money to find a better business mentor. As the saying goes, "Be careful what you wish for; you just might get it."

The truth of this saying was introduced to me by Esther and Jerry Hicks in their book, *The Law of Attraction*, which is on my recommended "must read" list. The universal principle that we attract to us what we focus on has been a significant revelation to me.

I had to this point in my life pretty much attracted by default everything in my personal experience. I at first strongly resisted the personal accountability of this fact, following the belief that God bestowed on us our experience based on whether or not we were following "the rules."

What a wakeup call! To learn that my experience was a result of what I broadcasted energetically into the "field." This knowledge was very exciting and scary as hell! Sure, the bad things in my experience were not fun, but on the other side of the coin, what if I could engineer my life? What if I could learn to create by intention, instead of reaping the results of my attraction by default? This negative karma-like attraction created a hodgepodge of experience, most of which I would not rationally choose with anything closely resembling a sane mind.

I had asked for a teacher and the teacher had appeared. "When the student is ready, the teacher will appear." I had created the learning experience I had so greatly desired. What I do with that gift is indeed entirely up to me.

Since then, my lessons and experiences with Jackson have continued to unfold. I am so thankful for his patient tutoring. I am sure he shakes his head and chuckles at my impetuousness and impatience. But I am also sure he values our friendship as much as I do. His patience matches his wisdom, and patience is a very useful trait for those interacting with me. I tend to be a "bottom line" kind of guy. I also have a bad habit of speaking or acting before my wisdom shifts into gear. But I am learning the wisdom of speaking less and leading by example, and thankfully, my friends assure me I am making progress.

"'Tis better to remain silent and be thought a fool than to open one's mouth and remove all doubt."
— Abraham Lincoln

One of my favorite quotes is "Do not spend any time trying to convince anyone of anything. Because if they are not asking, your answers are only irritating." I carry this quote with me in my wallet at all times. I periodically have to rewrite it on a new piece of paper when the paper falls apart with age. I have memorized it, but I'm still working on practicing it.

"Walk softly and carry a big lesson by example."
— Perry Chinn

Hey, I kind of like that! You heard it here first!

SECTION
3

ACCOUNTABILITY

9

RISING ABOVE THE VICTIM IDENTITY

"But unlike a kite, there is no string attached to how high and how far your goals may take you. They are limited only by the power of your imagination and the strength of your desire."
— Denis Waitley

We live in a society that celebrates the victim. Welfare mentality is king. Like the decadent Roman society of two thousand years ago, many people feel entitled to everything and clamor to be entertained and fed. We scream for our government welfare checks, our drugs, and our varied forms of mindless entertainment. We riot when it is rumored that federal support will be cut, while in the same breath we moan about and criticize the level of government interference and the insane levels of tax we pay.

Accountability seems to be a rare commodity. It is always someone else's fault and we are quick to point the finger, many times to culprits far beyond America's borders.

We are fighting numerous wars around the globe, motivated by greed, avarice, and bigotry. Our legal system is second to none in the world in terms of largess, abuse, and outright larceny.

Where is this coming from? What is the cause of this insanity?

It is really fairly simple. All of this ugliness can be traced to the ravings and whining of our fear-mind. Chester and his kind exist on the neediness of our fear-associated mind. If this fear-mind is left unattended and unobserved, there is no end to the devastation created.

If we speak out against the insanity, we are labeled unpatriotic. If we demand accountability in Washington and threaten special interests, we stand the risk of personal attack.

The statesman Cicero stood up against the weaknesses of ancient Rome by living as an example of the alternative. He practiced passive resistance. When he was pressed for an opinion, he spoke out; however, he knew the wisdom of refraining from attack. He understood that attacking "evil," however "right" it seemed, was still a method of the fear-mind.

Cicero overcame by example. And he was murdered for it. The fear-minds in power in his day could not bear to have such a threat in their midst.

Are we as fearless and noble today? Do we set an example by standing up against the injustice America seems so willing to be known for today? Our country is currently responsible for oppression and misery around the world that is shameful and embarrassing. What is our personal level of contribution?

Until recently, I belonged to a local service organization. After nearly twenty years, I finally concluded that my participation was a bit hypocritical. This group was and is very conservative, nationalistic, and sometimes righteously insensitive to human rights. The organization nevertheless prided itself (and continues to) upon all the "good" it does in the world. This "good" is indeed debatable and will be of considerable interest to historians someday.

One gentleman in the group is a retired politician. He is very distinguished, tall, eloquent, and generally well-respected. A few years ago when he was serving as the group's president, he and his wife hosted an afternoon potluck at their home. I will never forget the decorations in one corner of their kitchen. It was in effect a not so small shrine dedicated to our patriotic involvement in the Iraq conflict. The collection included photos of George W. Bush and their son, an air force pilot. The flags and bunting were really quite impressive. But to me, it felt oppressive and left me with an eerie feeling.

Over the years, this man was typically the one to initiate the more harsh nationalistic and "patriotic" sentiments in our weekly meetings. His prayers were strikingly one-sided. God bless America and protect our troops—requests made while we were the chief contributor to some of the most horrific human rights abuses on the planet, all in the name of the "War on Terror."

As the ugliness and lack of integrity concerning our involvement in the Middle East has become glaringly apparent over the past few years, his voice has become increasingly quieter. I no longer get his Bible-thumping, flag-waving e-mails. If anything, I feel his acute bewilderment and confusion. "We were right, but everything is falling apart!"

We have been duped on a national scale by the fear-initiated insanity of our collective Chester. Widespread fear has persuaded the most respected nation on earth to commit the most ugly and reprehensible acts. We are experiencing the collective pain of these actions. Our nation is spiritually sick and paying the awful price for the abandonment of our once noble ideals.

I thought I would share with you the prayer I wrote for my Rotary club at a time when we were deeply embroiled in the Iraq conflict:

My Prayer

My prayer today is not to an exclusive God,

One interested in the affairs of one favored country or government.

My prayer is for unity and understanding among all who breathe the air I breathe,

To and for all who smile at the questions of a child and those who feel warmth when extending the hand of friendship to another.

I pray today that service motivated by fear is a thing of the past and that understanding and tolerance is the language of my life and the source of my action.

This prayer I breathe on the eve of new hope and healing for our country and world.

AMEN!

The room was quiet after I prayed this prayer. I could feel that many were struggling with the concept that all the earth's citizens share a common goal. Peace.

I gave this prayer in the presence of many very conservative and "patriotic" folks—people more interested in the American brand of justice than forgiveness and understanding.

Where are we in the world today? Is the story all bad? Have we gone too far? Has our country lost what little credibility it had left? I don't believe so, even in light of the ongoing events around the world. The move toward spiritual consciousness is accelerating. More people are opening their eyes to the danger of identification with the fear-mind.

You and I can repair the damage, one brick at a time. By each one of us observing his or her personal Chester, we contribute to the reduction of the collective insanity. This is how healing begins. First with me, and then with the world.

This process will take time. It will require a level of contrition and humility long absent from our national policy. It will take all of us. It will require our quiet voice of responsibility to reach our leaders in our nation's capital.

In the twentieth century, Gandhi overcame the most powerful occupying presence on the planet (the British empire) by his use of passive resistance and spiritual consciousness. He did not fire a gun; he overcame by the strength of his presence. Gandhi understood the lure and danger of the fear-mind. He also intimately understood the power of quiet presence.

The challenge we face in this country is not to be taken in by those who are motivated by fear. Our country is in a transition. We have a tremendous opportunity to move forward with acceptance rather than with force. But it will require participating in a whole new mind-set.

"We can't solve problems by using the same kind of thinking we used when we created them."

— **Albert Einstein**

At the meltdown of our economy in 2008, the outgoing Federal Reserve chairman Alan Greenspan was said to be at a total loss as to why the financial tragedy had occurred. It made no sense to the group of people who had created the insanity. They were still thinking and acting out of the same antiquated fear-based mind-set.

Presence and a heightened level of "common sense" and observation of fear will be required as we navigate this new world and new century. We can no longer afford the luxury of burying our heads in the proverbial sand and hoping everything will be all right and return to "normal."

New thinking and courses of action are required of us and our children. Otherwise, we may see that spiritual consciousness will choose another path. Human existence may be relegated to the halls of the cosmic museum as a great experiment that "just didn't work out."

Will you join me in my intention of correcting the insanity? We can do it, one step at a time.

10

NURTURING SPIRIT

"Nurture your mind with great thoughts, for you will never go any higher than you think."
— **Benjamin Disraeli**

The Good News

I had a dream that I was a hawk. That I could soar high on the wind, flying wherever the currents took me. I had no limits; there were no ties to the earth restricting my ability to be where I willed or to see what I wanted to see.

My Native American animal totem is the red-tailed hawk. When my friend Bob Trask was thinking of the appropriate spirit totem for me, he did not have to spend much time at all selecting this powerful bird. I identify strongly with many characteristics of my feathered friends, particularly the hawk and eagle. Flying is freeing to me, therapy for a soul too often tied to earthly, mundane tasks and responsibilities. Nothing on this earth is quite like the experience of flight. I recall fondly the first flight following my achievement of solo status. The feeling of freedom, vision, and of just being alive was incredible!

Can you imagine for a moment being a hawk or eagle that believed it could not fly? Talk about hell on earth! How miserable would that bird's existence be if it were prevented from its most innate ability, flight? To me, that would be despair at its deepest level!

As a hawk is meant to soar and fly, you are a spiritual being who was not intended to be bound by the fears that today fill our minds and daily thoughts. Our spirits were created to fly high and free like the hawk, not scratch along in the dust like chickens.

I remember well an experience my wife and I had several years ago in that rather turbulent time soon after our marriage. We were both recently divorced and newly married to each other. We had begun attending weekly meetings at a church a few miles from our home, a church whose pastor was a very nice and well-meaning man. We both liked his sermons and were attempting to find some common ground spiritually and philosophically with a church group.

The incident that turned out to be the deal-breaker happened one Sabbath morning in a small group of about fifteen people. The subject being discussed was whether we individually felt assured of salvation. Did we "know" we were going to heaven? I remember the anticipation vibrating from my wife's direction as we began the discussion. This subject was very important to her. She had shared with me that one of the primary attractions she felt toward me when we first met was that I was a man connected with Source who had a Knowing of who he was and where he was going.

As the talking and sharing moved around the circle, it became apparent that most of those present had some very deep-rooted questions concerning their personal assurance of salvation. In fact, to my wife's amazement, not one person in the circle could say, without a doubt, that he or she felt "saved" or that his or her name was written in the "Book of Life."

This lack of spiritual confidence baffled Melanie to no end, but to me this was nothing new. She could not understand how it was possible all these spiritual people, in this very spiritual place, could be anything less than one hundred percent confident in their spiritual nature. Wasn't the purpose of religion and church to raise our spiritual consciousness and understanding? Wasn't the goal to lift ourselves above the fear and insecurity of life to a solid knowing of our connection to divinity and Source? How is it that people can spend their entire lives in a church and not feel an assurance of salvation?

What a shame to be born a hawk and not be empowered with the gift of flight! To have all of the equipment, innately, and not know the feeling of the air beneath your wings—Torture!

The crazy thing is that the church, and I am not being critical here of any specific denomination, is commonly thought

203

of as THE place where you can commune with fellow spiritual "flyers." This is where we were promised the opportunity to soar in spirit and love!

But to look around and one day realize that most of those inhabiting the pews do not know their spiritual nature and birthright is disconcerting to say the least and at most, very sad.

We are spiritual beings enjoying the privilege of a physical experience. It makes no more sense to have to explain that to someone than it would be to have to explain to a fish that he can swim! Spiritual is what we are, not what we become! Somehow we have gotten the idea that we are hawks without wings, and fish that do not know how to swim!

Spiritual is our very nature. Divinity is our essence. Thoughts of anything less are an illusion. The challenge is our journey back to realization of who we are—to knowing we are complete spiritually and that no thing is missing other than our knowing.

The Bible says, "All have sinned and have come short…." What can this mean? How can you define sin and still retain the dignity of knowing who you are?

To me, sin is a belief—it doesn't matter how the belief was acquired—that I am separate from my Source. If the hawk had an ego fear-mind, it might believe flight was impossible. Thankfully, our friends in the natural world have not been blessed with such a thing as the ego, the fear-mind. A hawk, by nature, flies. A fish, by nature, swims. Dolphins leap, kangaroos hop. No effort, no thought. It's who they ARE! Why must we believe we are anything other or less than who we are?

The only explanation for this insanity is fear and the idea that we are separate from our Source. I can find no other reason for this serious and unconscious malady that afflicts human beings.

The good news is that we can fly in a spiritual sense. And it is our nature to fly. The not-so-good news is that all too often we (as humans) have agreed upon a belief system that says we are incapable of flight.

So if our true nature is obscured by this fear-generated B.S. (belief system), how do we re-claim our birthright, particularly if we don't realize or understand that we have misplaced it?

It has been said that we each have a "God-shaped" void in ourselves that only God or Spirit can fill, and this emptiness, even when not understood, seeks for a solution, a filling. If we are spiritual by nature, which I believe/know we are, then at some deep level, no matter how fear-oppressed we are, we are drawn to re-connect and re-discover our identity. And that deep knowing will strive for an awakening. It must.

This striving for awakening can manifest in many different ways. It may be a search for completeness. In the unconscious state, a person will often try to complete self with a grasping for material things, or sex, or drugs. We may spend thousands of dollars and years of our life trying to find the right guru, religion, or cult. But there is really nothing to find. We are already complete. Just unaware, unconscious. Clueless.

The answer that resonates with my spirit is that we will create opportunities, usually through suffering, to re-connect with Source. These self-created crises are opportunities for awakening. However, if the ego is allowed to take center stage in our self-identity, understanding and awakening will be frustrated, blocked, and may not come. It will at least be delayed. Chester will keep the noise level of our lives at a level sufficient to obscure that awakening. But the void must be filled, so suffering will continue to be created until the pain reaches the critical point of surrender.

"Nurturing self does not exclude God; it discovers God."
— Perry Chinn

Surrender

As a student of understanding, and one offering myself up to opportunities of enlightenment, I am beginning to follow the wise practice of listening to my wife. "It is time to write your book," she informed me a few months ago. This directive was not issued from any personal agenda of hers, or to promote the lofty literary goals of her beloved husband. No, the reason for her request was simple. Her good friend was in trouble. Yep, you probably guessed it. A case of an unenlightened male. My wife's favorite walking partner was beyond frustration with her husband. It was apparent, from the brief description of his level of reactivity that he was suffering from a high degree of spiritual unconsciousness and identification with his fear-mind.

I felt and understood his pain. I remember a funny little "How To" book about approaching fatherhood, where in the opening credits of the book, the author gave his most credible credentials as follows: "I have raised my children to adulthood without becoming an ax-murderer." I was impressed. I consider that quite an accomplishment, considering I now have raised several young ones through the teenage years.

Navigating the often bumpy path to personal awareness can be almost as daunting a task as raising a teenager. It looks simple from a distance, but then so does juggling torches.

My advice, given to my wife to share with her friend, was to see whether her husband was willing to look at the fear-mind issues. This was a risk of course because obviously his fear-mind was in control of his reasoning. About the best we can do is wait for a window of opportunity. Let the student create enough pain to be ready to receive the lesson.

Just as fighting the darkness by beating it senseless with a torch is futile, so fighting fear is equally non-productive. Our job as a friend is not to react, but to wait, observe, and be on hand when the other is ready. Only awareness can manage and eventually erase the control and tyranny of the fear-mind.

When is a person ready to receive understanding? When he is so tired of the pain and suffering that he has no ego-energy left to fight the arrival of consciousness.

That is when he reaches the important moment of surrender.

When most people consider the concept of surrender, they often associate the meaning of the word with failing or just giving up. But from a spiritual perspective, to surrender is actually very powerful.

Surrender, at least in consideration of the ego, is nothing more than non-reactivity to the actions of our fear-mind, Chester. We are in a beautiful state of surrender when Chester is sitting quietly on his stool in the corner. There is no drama. There is no pain. Only quiet observation.

When activity is required, it is not motivated by fear, but energized by the calm knowing of your aware self. Chester is not involved in this process unless intentionally invited.

"All suffering is ego created and is due to resistance."
— **Eckhart Tolle**

Are we resisting our innate need to reconnect with Source by our connection and identification with our fear-mind?

With surrender, usually at a point of profound exhaustion, a space is created. This space allows for the recognition of the ego form. Chester emerges from the mist of your swirling emotions. He is discovered for the interfering presence he is. Of course, Chester will immediately begin pointing the finger of blame outside himself to any number of available causes. "The devil made me do it," or "I can't help it; I was born that way," or "I was pushed to my limit." There is no shortage of external causative factors to which Chester will try to shift accountability.

If, after exhaustion, surrender, and the subsequent creation of space, your awakened self has the consciousness to choose a higher level of accountability, spiritual healing will occur. With accountability for the true cause of unconsciousness comes the mature calmness of observing rather than the insanity of reacting. This task is not easy to accomplish! Our roots and habits of reaction run very deep. Even with weeks and months of apparent "smooth sailing" in non-reaction, one small event can trigger a very ugly tantrum. This can be very discouraging, particularly when the ego has partnered in your "enlightenment." Monitoring your emotions, which are the indicators of your thoughts, requires constant attention. Do not underestimate the craftiness of Chester, nor his desire to regain control of thought and response. Observe. Breathe. Smile at Chester. With time you will be able to anticipate his emotional triggers and remove the critical element in the succession of reactive events.

For a fire to burn out of control, fuel must be present, and in adequate supply. Remove your fear response by remaining the observer and Chester's plans will starve for lack of fuel.

Surrender: Accept the present moment. Remind yourself that Chester's world is either in the future or the past. There are either problems to be solved in some future time or insults to worry about in the past. This is fuel for Chester's fire. By surrendering to what is Now, you place Chester back on his stool and allow peace back into your life.

Many may feel that surrender is giving up. Far from it. Surrender is refusing to resist. Surrender is refusing to continue to beat your proverbial head against the wall. The power that comes with non-resistance will attract all that is needed for you.

Jim Carrey's character in *Bruce Almighty* demonstrates surrender for me very well. Jim is playing a guy named Bruce who is fed up with the injustice in his life. He is tired of being on God's shit list.

So he calls Him on it. He dares to call God accountable for the suffering he sees in the world. And God answers.

He gives Bruce a taste of being God. He shows Bruce in the ensuing series of escapades that being God is not all it is cracked up to be. Bruce realizes that joy is truly uncaused. That true happiness is allowing, not forcing. Bruce is finally able to surrender to the state of presence and allowing.

What fuels the fear response for your Chester and frustrates your process of surrender? Is it the movies you watch, the conversations you participate in, maybe it is the church you attend? Is it fear of a terrorist attack, fear of a stock market collapse, fear of lack in any form? Does the environment you choose to nourish and participate in support the belief of your complete Self or does it support your belief in lack and fear?

We may not, at least initially, have much control of our emotionally charged fear-responses. This is largely due to our lack of, or very low levels of, consciousness. However, with even a little awareness, we do have an increasing level of control of our personal environment. What we read, hear, smell, touch, and participate in, is within our power of choice.

One of the most powerful influences in our environment is the people with whom we associate. When we awaken to observing, we will have an increased opportunity to keep our space clean and sacred. What is the level of accountability and consciousness of the people in your church, your social club, your work? Are there family members who rob us of spiritual focus? Are we nurturing relationships with friends who steal more spiritual energy than they contribute?

It may be time in your life to do some selective pruning. Now may be a great opportunity to clean out the closet, so to speak, within your circle of friends and among those with whom you hang out. Is it worth it to you in the bigger picture? There are obviously more tactful ways of cleaning up your space; however, sometimes you just have to be able to say "No," or "enough is enough."

Do not let another person pour toxic waste into your personal pool. This is serious business. It is a matter of incredible consequence in your level of happiness and spiritual health. This experience, this life is indeed too short to waste on an existence of fear-induced unconsciousness.

If the offenders are family members or spouses, the task is more difficult. The fear of holding them accountable and asking them to respect your environment may keep many from addressing the problem. Often it may require some form of "tough love." What is usually helpful is a direct form of communication that clearly establishes your boundaries. Of course, this is not easy, but the reward can be incalculable.

The reality is that some of us will not see our Chester in this lifetime. Why this is so is a mystery to me; however, it is a testament to the awesome privilege of choice based on awareness. Do we choose before this life experience whether we will awaken in this physical experience? And if we do not, is it really a choice if we are not conscious enough to make a choice? Good questions! Still working on the answer to that one!

There are times when I wonder whether awareness is a blessing or a curse. The pain often associated with spiritual growth (or at least my version of it!) is at times hard to endure. My good friend Bob Trask has stated that "Pain is inevitable; however, suffering is optional." My interpretation of that statement is "Don't let Chester be the interpreter for the events in your life!" If Chester creates pain and drama, the only conclusion will be suffering! Fuel for Chester!

What I do know is there is no going back. There is no stuffing the genie back in the bottle! Knowledge is power and awareness is spiritual knowing and opportunity for peace. Chester will do his best to try to convince me he knows all this "stuff" and not to get overly concerned or excited about it. This is his not so subtle way of trying to sweep the issue of consciousness under the proverbial carpet. Your challenge is to be aware to the point of calling Chester on his B.S.!

Understanding Fear and Its Impact on the Body

Our positive and negative beliefs not only impact our health but also every aspect of our life. When we truly recognize that our beliefs are that powerful, we hold the key to freedom.

"You can live a life of fear or live a life of love. You have the choice! But I can tell you that if you choose to see a world full of love, your body will respond by growing in health."
— Bruce Lipton, Ph.D.

For our fear-based mind to be able to survive, it must create or be in agreement with a belief system of physical being. When we are identified with form or ego, our self must be able to have a relative constant for being. Just like a ship must have a bearing and a known fixed position, our physical self must have a known belief system to navigate the world of form.

If I were to ask the next person I meet on the street whether he or she preferred to experience the blessing of a wellness infused body as opposed to an ill one, most likely the answer would be "Yes!" But interestingly, if I followed up that question with asking the person questions about self-care including his/her nutrition, exercise, and preventive habits such as dental hygiene, chiropractic, and meditation, most people would begin acting very nervous and defensive about why they were not caring for themselves. Accountability and the Law of Attraction again.

The sad truth is that very few people are consistently proactive in self-care from a physical standpoint. The number of people in the U.S. considered to be obese is now well over half. Childhood obesity is not only a serious problem but an impending national catastrophe, making such minor issues as funding Social Security and Medicare seem almost trivial by comparison.

Sedentary habits in the workplace and particularly in the home are diminishing vitality and creativity. Exercise is the domain of the "healthy crowd" not the "regular Joe." One of the most common answers I get when inquiring about the exercise habits of a patient is "Well, Doc, I do walk from my car to the office, and I use the stairs sometimes." Bottom line, the regular regimen of exercise is consistently absent.

Equally a problem is our typical American concept of prevention. Usually, that consists of injecting a chemical into our bodies and expecting wellness as a result. Or maybe a yearly visit to the dentist. And hey, don't expect me to floss or even brush my teeth everyday! Oh, and don't even start with me about those chiropractors! They just want to keep you coming back to get all your money!

Basically, most of us exist in the crisis-motivated mode. The "If it ain't broke—don't fix it!" paradigm of personal care. That's fine if we are willing to accept the eventual result of later having to pay a big repair bill! And that's assuming repair is even possible when we have created a crisis large enough to motivate a trip to the gym, chiropractor, or dentist.

What keeps us from being proactive? Fear and the deep sleep of unconsciousness. Fear is a great motivator, particularly in a crisis mentality. Fear is also a great paralyzer. We fail to engage in action that will potentially benefit us, and instead, only motivate ourselves in an environment of fear. Like a background noise of which we eventually become unaware, the constant baseline of fear infuses our actions and thoughts.

Bruce Lipton's work on the physiological effects on the cell in the environment of fear is very enlightening. The negative effects on our wellness due to living with fear are devastating. As we are the Creators of our experience, so we are the creators of our physical expression. We have the opportunity to create our health and wellness. We are not victims. Therefore, it would make sense to do all we can to rid ourselves of fear and its negative physiological and spiritual effects.

Remember what we learned about Chester and fear? He eats fear for breakfast! And for lunch and dinner, AND he eats between meals!

Our fear-mind, if allowed to thrive with self-identification, will consume large quantities of fear-fuel. And if not provided with readily available fuel, Chester will be happy to set up his own fear factories and supply lines, and he will create any of an infinite variety of means to feed his voracious appetite.

The antidote for this destructive process is presence. Simple observation created from a gap of awareness is all that is necessary to see how the fear-motivated ego reacts. You can become more acutely aware of Chester's tricks. It really is that simple. The hard part is disconnecting your identification with Chester. I am not saying this is necessarily easy, but it can be done, and it takes only as long as you need it to take. How long is this pain necessary in my life? As Eckhart Tolle says, "as long as necessary...."

Would you knowingly and willingly put on a bathing suit and go swimming in an open cesspool or sewer? Probably not, yet the vast majority of humanity not only "swim" in an immense pool of fear, but also contribute daily to filling the pool! This is truly amazing when you stop for a moment to look at this phenomenon. We are slowly killing ourselves with fear, yet we are the ones filling the pool with noxious poison, putting the gun to our heads and pulling the trigger!

Several years ago, during one of Bob Trask's retreats on Molokai in Hawaii, I was privileged to lead twenty or so people on a hike to a sacred pool at the head of the Halawa valley on the eastern end of the island of Molokai.

I remember the day. Warm sun, beautiful green foliage, immense trees and azure blue water. After parking the cars at the trailhead, we left the ocean and followed the path up the valley. We passed through dark canopies of huge trees and green twisting vines. We followed low rock walls built hundreds of years earlier by the original Polynesian settlers of this sacred valley. After an hour or so of fairly easy walking, we eventually reached a series of waterfalls and intervening pools of clear, cool water. The soothing mist from the falls and the pleasant sound of water pounding and swirling on the rocks was the perfect reward for the hike up the valley. Unable to resist the water, several of us finally shed our clothes and went for a swim in the pool. What a treat! We spent a couple of hours eating lunch, laughing, sharing stories, and relaxing. Later in the afternoon, refreshed and happy, we headed back down the trail toward the ocean and our cooler full of cold watermelon.

What a different experience it would have been if we had arrived at the pool only to find cigarette butts floating and bobbing on the surface, or submerged beer cans, maybe even effluent pipes pouring sewage into the basin below the falls, garbage carelessly tossed in. What was once a wonderful and soothing experience would have become intolerable.

Just like our shared responsibility to keep our world clean and litter free, we also have a responsibility to keep our personal "pool" or mental habitation clean. The thoughts we think, of course, are in our control—especially as we awaken to more awareness and understand the direct and inevitable connection between what we think, emotionally engage in, and then experience.

What may be even more dramatic is the connection between what we allow into our personal space and what we experience. I think we have all experienced the unpleasant feeling of another person invading "our space." Another's face pressed into ours when uninvited can be very uncomfortable. It is not only the physical intrusion, but even more the "energy" the person projects into our environment. If we do not guard our space with intention and awareness, pollution of our energetic field will be the inevitable result.

But how can we interact with the world and yet keep our pool clean? How can we be "in the world" of ego, yet not "of the world" of fear.

People will bring into your pool a cloud of fear, unless your awareness, your "energy field" is of sufficient strength. Remember Pigpen from the *Peanuts* cartoon? His cloud of dirt follows him everywhere he goes. People create and clothe themselves in fear in much the same way. They carry it along with them, polluting and contaminating any who do not consciously safeguard their personal space.

This energetic personal hygiene can be accomplished with tact and love. However, it may have to be tough love at times, depending on the strength of the other's fear cloud. Egoistic fear can be both overwhelming and seductive. If a person engages another's fear with his own, the result is only more fear, and more identification with the person's fear creator, his own Chester.

Robert Fulghum tells the story of a man nearly burned to death in his own bed. When the fireman asks him how the fire started, the man replies, "I don't know! It was on fire when I laid down on it!"

We create, participate in, breathe, exhale, distribute, and boast in the language of fear. And we will until we each personally create enough pain to open a window to see Chester for who he is. With that seeing comes an opportunity to get out of the pool and truly live.

Do you remember what joy feels like? You might say, "I have never known joy." My answer, however, is that of course you have known Joy! You are, in essence, pure joy. You have just forgotten. Watch a two year old at play for a few minutes. That is joy. Before you learned to swim in fear, you LIVED in joy. Not only can you remember the joy, but you have the opportunity to return to that life experience. First, you just have to learn how to observe and tame your Chester.

Take an afternoon and go to a park or mall play area and watch some children at play. Observe. See the joy. Especially the younger ones, before they acquire the fear and the sense of separateness. Is it because they are so young and you are…not so young? No, it isn't the age difference; it's the fear difference.

Watch a dog at play with his owner. Pure joy. No Chester-in-the-head paralyzing and obscuring the joy. Of course, the dog has a natural fear defense mechanism. If a larger dog shows up, caution will cause the dog's behavior to change, but what I'm referring to is that the dog doesn't have a fear-mind—it has no need to have conflict to maintain its identity. If you choose to keep Chester seated on his stool and well-behaved, then joy, not fear, will be the flavor of your life.

A very common malady in people today is the errant belief that completeness and wholeness is somehow found outside of Self. The church teaches that we are flawed, incomplete, and separate from the source of Go(o)d. What would it be like if our young people were raised with a sense of knowing they were complete? That does not, in my opinion, take away from the understanding that there is maturing and growth to experience. But if children can be taught and shown by example that they are a complete from day one, what a difference it would make in their journeys to spiritual understanding. The truth is that in many ways, they are more "complete" as infants than they are as ego-identified adults.

Our society tends to imply that "completeness" is found in pursuing the material. The current designer clothes, the bigger, more powerful car, the more "bling" all combine to contribute to a greater sense of being and self. However, the "bloom is coming off the rose" so to speak. More and more people are stumbling upon a higher vibration of consciousness that is inconsistent with the retailers' propaganda. And that fact has the commercial world running scared. Nevertheless, the world is transitioning from material-based completeness of the self to an understanding that self is inherently complete and that relationships are the new currency of abundance.

On the subject of physical health, I would venture to say that all illness is fear in physical form. If I choose to live at the highest level of accountability, I cannot become a victim. And that includes a victim of illness. Now of course, we have a functional immune response and our body is constantly adapting to its environment, so symptoms will come and go as our body dynamically responds to our physical world. But this is not "sick." This is in fact "wellness." Being sick is an agreement with fear, a declared mistrust of our body's innate ability to maintain a functional balance in relation to our outside world.

Being "sick" is resistance. Being "sick" is fear. Allow your body to "speak" its language and do what it does best. Being at war with symptoms is like shooting the messenger before he can get down from his horse. Allowing your body to express its symptoms without the judgment of "being sick" is an incredibly liberating experience.

You are able to see that the authentic "you" cannot be "sick." It cannot be less than one hundred percent. Let Chester be sick. He is good at it. What you will find is that without your attention, illness has no reward. Much like a child misbehaving to achieve a parent's reaction, with no reaction, the illness disappears on its own. But with reaction comes more "acting out" and of course more pain.

With the onset of your physical symptoms of illness, practice observation, self-presence, meditation, and non-reactivity. You will be pleasantly surprised at how your body responds. Observing decreases and eventually dissipates the resistance, much like the sun evaporating the morning fog. Breathe. Center. Observe.

Try not to punish yourself for being sick. Look for the opportunity to lean more about how your body responds to stress and fear identification. With increased personal knowledge and understanding comes a better knowing of how to prevent illness.

When I give health talks to my patients and other groups of people, I absolutely love to speak about the incredible miracle of the body that we each inhabit.

Did you know that our human body produces over eight million red blood cells every second? For each of these little miracles to happen, thousands of organic chemical reactions must occur at just the appropriate time and in the exact sequence. Multiply this mind-boggling achievement second after second throughout your lifetime and the enormity of this task quickly leaves our feeble thinking mind in the dust. And this is just one small fraction of the orchestrated building and healing going on in our body!

The one plus one equals two understanding of how the human body works simply can't keep pace with how our internal universe works. Science cannot explain it, and at best we can only guess at how this process continues day in and day out. Not to mention the mind-stopping question of how it all got started.

The world of science is just now beginning to think "outside the box" of Newtonian and Einsteinian knowledge. We are starting to appreciate the importance of our physical and spiritual environment and the resulting impact on our health.

Years ago, in my first practice, I had purchased a Chevy Suburban. My initial reason for buying such a large beast was due to our growing family and the enormous task of just hauling stuff around. I had the idea to use the rear windows of the truck as a sort of traveling billboard. The graphic designer did a great job of putting a spine and my clinic information in vinyl across the rear window. The quote I used at the time as my office tagline was "The Power that Made the Body, Heals the Body."

I would frequently get comments from people that they thought the line meant something religious, when my intention was to point out the amazing ability of the human body to heal, particularly with a minimum of interference. It surprised me how many people thought I was advertising for my church and not my business.

One danger of the scientific method of attempting to understand the body is that we tend to reduce the physical aspect of ourselves into a collection of parts. Parts that are separate functional entities. With this tendency toward "parts is parts" thinking comes the minimizing of the miracle as a whole.

Natural or "whole"-istic healing attempts to utilize the best of both worlds. When we need the wonders of technology to stitch us back together, to repair broken bones, to give our body a chance to heal, we can utilize these valuable tools and still respect the holistic, whole body "science" of Spirit.

I am currently preparing to release a food supplement product based on the amino acid L-arginine. In 1998, three scientists discovered the link between L-arginine and the natural release of nitric oxide in the blood. Nitric oxide has been shown to assist in the reversal of the effects of atherosclerosis (hardening of the arteries), decreasing high blood pressure and generally improving the circulation of blood throughout the body.

These scientists received the 1998 Nobel Prize for physiology and medicine for this significant discovery. Some of this research was directed into the pharmaceutical industry with significant results in the area of male sexual enhancement; however, the more exciting results (I suppose it depends on your point of view) have been in the holistic, natural food supplement industry.

Many studies have shown that people who take this supplement experience dramatic positive effects in such areas as the terrible side effects of diabetes, blood pressure normalization, and a significant decrease in heart disease and stroke.

My goal for our cardiovascular formula is primarily for the people of Asia. Diabetes and its lethal complications are now considered to be the primary causes of death in China. Heart disease is a close second. I understand that the typical "high end" evening-out meal in urban China is now the Chinese version of Pizza Hut and McDonalds. Complete with a *maitre d'*.

Sadly, Asians seem to be emulating what they perceive as the West's success. To a large degree, they have copied our health care and dietary protocols. And now their people are reaping the results. Cardiovascular disease, diabetes, and autoimmune disorders are sweeping across areas of the world where until recently these diseases were rare.

China is inhabited by almost one and a half billion people, people with a savings rate of over fifty percent, with most of this money shipped overseas to finance our excess. Our lifestyle, directly and indirectly, is sustained by our Chinese friends. And to thank them, we are helping them destroy their health. My goal is to help reverse this cardiovascular time bomb. This is no small task, but we have to start somewhere.

Because the science and results of this Nobel Prize winning discovery have been largely ignored by traditional medicine, they remain largely unknown to the general population.

Why? Because natural food supplements don't support the pharmaceutical industry. Being perhaps the largest single political special interest lobby in Washington, D.C., the drug (legalized) industry is a moneymaker. More holistic avenues of health improvement don't typically make the news.

Each year, several hundred thousand people die from the negative effects of drugs and surgery. We are the most medicated nation on the planet, consuming vast amounts of prescription drugs each year. Our infant mortality rate would be shameful even for a Third World country. Childhood and adolescent obesity is at epidemic proportions. In another twenty-five years, diabetes is expected to increase by almost three hundred and fifty percent. We are literally killing ourselves with our "healthy" ignorance.

Okay, for balance let's have some good news. Medical technology has made tremendous leaps in knowledge and understanding. Acute trauma surgical techniques are nothing less than astounding. If I were to be in a helicopter crash tomorrow (and survive), I wouldn't want to be anywhere else in the world when it comes to emergency care and medicine.

But can these accomplishments in technological medicine excuse our continued trend of ignorance when it comes to preventive health care and care of the whole body—true holistic wellness?

You would be helping yourself and your family immeasurably by using a little bit of common sense when it comes to health care decisions. Take a second look at the medication in your hand. We keep medications under lock and key mainly because if healthy people take medication not intended for them, sickness and even death can result. But how logical is it to expect that the same chemical given to a sick person will bring him or her back to health?

Granted, some emergency situations require aggressive and even dangerous intervention. But the fact remains, we are drugging ourselves senseless, and our society is among the sickest on the planet.

How is it we have become so drug-laced as a people? Think about the fear element for a moment. What motivates most people to take a potentially harmful chemical? Could it be fear?

My wife and I were just chuckling and shaking our heads over a television advertisement earlier this evening. It was a new "supplemental" drug, meaning it is to be given in addition to the "normally prescribed medication," recommended for those suffering depression. Like most drug commercials, the first few seconds portrayed well-dressed, happy looking people, free from the ravages of depression. But most of the commercial was dedicated to the rapid-fire oral warnings of the potential side effects. Suicide, intentional tremors, seizures, and coma inducement were just a few of the potential effects of taking this medication. And the original target symptom for the drug was just plain old depression!

Here is a radical concept: how about getting outside and taking a walk? Or involving yourself in a community activity or service? All of these have been shown to be much more effective than any chemically induced benefits! But we take the drugs. We want the effect NOW. We place our drug industry on a pedestal and viciously defend our right to receive medication.

Have you followed the health care debates lately? What is most vociferously defended? Access to low cost drugs.

Our society has spent billions searching for cancer's cause. Science is convinced that the "cancer bug" or some etiological agent will someday be discovered. Maybe.

Deepak Chopra, a widely respected medical doctor, made a rather strong statement a few years ago. He said, "Illness is never the result of bacteria or virus; it is always the result of a susceptible host." Hmmm….Why would he say that?

Like the saying goes, "It takes two to tango." The germ theory is fine as long as you don't forget that we have an immune system as well. There must be a susceptible host in order for the "germ" to create the "disease." It is a synergistic dynamic. The weaker the host, the easier it will be for the dis-ease process to gain a foothold.

Could it be that health is more the result of a healthy immune system and our ability to adapt and synergistically coexist with our environment than it is a result of the drugs we take?

Again, in emergency situations, drugs can be lifesavers. But I think you would agree that today we have gone way past the point of excess.

I counsel my patients on a good balance between exercise, whole food use, and occasional supplementation, along with regular chiropractic care, massage, acupuncture, and non-invasive health disciplines. Save the drugs for the emergency room where they belong.

A 1970s study showed that several test groups receiving regular chiropractic care had an immune response that was between two hundred and four hundred percent more powerful than those not under chiropractic maintenance care. No, this study wasn't some backwater collection of data from a couple of chiropractors in Arkansas. This was the Pero study backed by Yale University.

Our bodies know what works. We know when we are suppressing the body's natural health and immune response, but we want and demand the immediate effects of the drugs. Please don't ask me to wait for my body to heal!

Do we then whine and complain when our health deteriorates and we want the government or our health provider to save us, or do we take the mature road of accountability and place the responsibility for our health where it belongs? ON the medicine cabinet (in the mirror, dude, not inside it in the bottles).

My wife is justifiably worried when I end up stepping on more toes than I potentially enlighten minds. Please understand that I sincerely care for you and your health. My goal is increased knowledge, awareness, and joy in our lives. Encouraging fear is counterproductive to that goal. Chester would like to see motivation at the point of a spear of fear. Our innate wisdom sees the folly of fear and the value of observation and knowing.

My attempt to inform will indeed challenge many belief systems. I can live with allowing people to get angry and stirred up if the result is a desire to change behavior. I have developed a pretty thick skin (and some would say head) over the years. You can't really be a true chiropractor without attracting a few thrown tomatoes. And I try not to take it personally, knowing it is the collective Chester who is threatened and the authentic Self being awakened when cherished belief systems are challenged.

You have been blessed to live in an age where the sum total of knowledge accumulated over thousands of years is no further away than your computer screen. When it comes to your health and your family's, you have no excuse when you have all these resources at your fingertips. Research these health trends for yourself. Take the responsibility that is yours alone. Find out what really contributes to health, well-being, and increased vitality of mind, body, and spirit. Be the token pain in the ass in your family. Be the obnoxious one at family picnics. In a loving and caring way of course!

When it comes to uncovering sensitive belief systems, Chester knows that awareness and accountability are both irritating and attractive. The shining light of Spirit both attracts people and scares them to death. The double-edged sword is that once we know, there is no turning back. Every time you swig back a drink full of chemically altered sweeteners, preservatives, and coloring, you will know you are playing a kind of long-term Russian roulette.

Most people (actually most Chesters) will never forgive you for shining the light on their closely held belief systems and accompanying ignorance. It is the unforgivable sin. You probably should have thought of this before picking up this book! (Maybe my next version of this book should come with a warning sticker!)

Please remember, the goal here is a life of joy. Not pain. No one wants to be a pariah in his household, community, or place of work. We can, by example, be that light of awareness. So when the opportunity to share is invited, be tactful and honor the timing of the other person's individual spiritual journey. Remember, unless people are asking, your answers will only be irritating. So just be present, observe, live your life as an example, and be ready to share and enlighten when you are asked.

The way of the peaceful warrior. Slay Chester with presence and kindness; leave your sword in its scabbard.

11

LEARNING ABOUT RISK

"A ship is safe in harbor, but that's not what ships are for."
— **William Shedd**

Taking the Risk

Music has always been one of my passions and a central part of my life. From a very young age, I have enjoyed listening to and creating music. My first instrument was the flutophone in second grade, and then I was encouraged to take up the saxophone. I still have a horn, and I do take it out occasionally, dust it off, and annoy the cat.

About ten years ago, I was kicked back on the sofa reading the Sunday paper when a small ad caught my eye. The Seattle Symphony Chorale was holding auditions. At that time, I knew next to nothing about classical music so I had little appreciation for it. But I have always loved challenges, so I was intrigued. A few years of singing in the local community choir was fulfilling to a degree, but I felt I could do more.

One of my patients, a retired airline captain, sang in the chorale and gave music lessons, so I decided to take a couple of lessons, pick his brain for advice, and go for the audition.

The auditions were held in a room at the Cornish College of Arts in Seattle and Dr. Fiore was the chorale director. I trembled as I sang my audition number and struggled through a few scales. Dr. Fiore kindly smiled and said, "How would you like to sing tenor?" I was stunned, but I somehow managed to mumble, "Yes, I would like that very much. Thank you."

A few weeks later, I joined about a hundred and twenty other folks at the season retreat. As the new kid in town, not knowing anyone, I was intimidated and a bit overwhelmed.

But then we began our warm-up. I still remember with goose bumps the sound of over a hundred voices coming together to form the most beautiful sound I have ever heard. I was home!

After ten years, I still head out every Monday evening after work to sing with the chorale and my friends at the symphony. I have learned to appreciate and love the classical masterpieces we are privileged to sing. To perform in such a talented group, in the midst of a world-class symphony, is indeed an honor and an incredible pleasure. And I am thankful for the huge risk I took to audition and the fear I had to put aside in order to experience it.

As I write these words we are preparing for another presentation of Beethoven's Ninth symphony, commonly referred to as *The Ode to Joy*. Each year as the holiday season approaches, I "joyously" anticipate this incredible event and increasingly appreciate the genius and spirit of Beethoven.

It was after several years of singing this piece with the Seattle Symphony and Chorale that I finally took the time to read carefully through the English translation of the German words we were performing. Our director, Joe Crnko, continually urges us to dive deep into the music, especially the translation and meaning of the words that we sing in so many languages. As we understand the meaning, our inflection, tone, and spirit is then shared to a much fuller extent with our audience.

In the opening lines of the choral movement, these words jumped out at me: *"Joy, thou shining spark of God…Your magic reunites those Whom stern custom has parted…"*

Joy is the magic that has healed my life. To know finally that I am not this fearful voice of Chester in my head, changed my life beyond measure. I saw that by removing the walls of fear, I could come to know the joy that is my very essence. The joy that reunites me with my brothers and sisters around this small world.

Please take some time to see the magic that is in and behind the eyes of the people with whom you share your life. As you learn to look beyond the fear in their eyes, you will discover the magic of joy that we all share. You will then begin to see in the other the shining spark of God that ties us all together.

Overcoming Procrastination

Fear will always handicap your ability to create with inspiration. Fear cancels inspiration. They are mutually exclusive. Look at times in your own life when your creative energies were in high gear. I would willingly bet good money that fear was far out of the picture. Fear and constructive creation cannot co-exist.

So if your goal is to write that book (this particular goal is REALLY scary!), rebuild that car in your garage, create that new business, the first task is to move beyond your fear. The goal here is not to fight or resist, but to move forward and beyond. Just as turning on the light in a dark room removes the illusion of dark, so the presence of inspired action evaporates fear.

Procrastination is also often a symptom of fear. Fear that your results will not be "good enough," fear someone else will criticize, not support, not understand. Or simply a fear of change. According to psychologists, change is one of the "top three" fears we have. So to prevent the fear and its pain, you avoid the opportunity.

To avoid the risk is paralysis. The remedy is action. One of my favorite sayings is, "It does not matter whether you are on the right track; if you are not moving, the train will run you down."

One of many misconceptions about action, and one that keeps many stuck in their tracks, is the fear of making a wrong decision or taking off in the "wrong" direction. But if change is an opportunity to risk and learn, maybe any risk is worth it?

What if there were no such thing as a wrong decision or wrong direction? That would then leave just a variety of "right" decisions, with varying degrees of learning opportunities and chances for exploration!

Choose action sprinkled with what wisdom you have attained to this point. The important thing is to MOVE! But not in a flurry of Chester-inspired insanity. Move through your paralysis with Source-inspired action. Observe Chester's tendency to charge off into the fray with guns blazing! Laugh a little at his expense. Then move through with intention and purpose!

It has taken me many years to get up the courage to write this book. I have been paralyzed by feelings of inadequacy as a writer, fears that no one would want to read a book I would write! Then finally, I realized I had nothing to lose and everything to gain! Confidence! Experience! And the reward of a published book to prepare the way for my life's work of sharing, speaking, teaching, and inspiring others to move through being stuck in their fears.

So I declared my freedom from fear! That is not to say that fear does not sneak around on occasion, but now it rules far less of my life. Chester is alive and well, just tamed with observance on his chair in the corner.

What inspires you? If you jumped out of bed tomorrow morning and with joy and energy entered the day eager to explore and create, what would you be doing? Would it be your current job? It could be, although it might look a bit different than your life today. What opportunities ignite passion in your life?

"Don't limit yourself. Many people limit themselves to what they think they can do. You can go as far as your mind lets you. What you believe, remember, you can achieve."
— Mary Kay Ash

Resolve not to waste one more day doing what fails to inspire you. Do what you love! And if doing what you love is absolutely not possible from your current position, whose responsibility is it to move you?

I mentioned before that my decision to move from the world of logging to becoming a chiropractor was a dramatic change in my life. A certain amount of security was associated with staying right where I was. But the bottom line was that I was playing someone else's game. It was time for me to create my own game. It was scary and my wife thought I was more than just a little crazy, but I knew I needed to create a new and different experience and path of opportunity in my life.

You are invited by Spirit to create something new in your life on a daily basis. And probably many times in each day. As you step away from fear, you will more easily recognize these opportunities as the gifts they are. You will slowly stop seeing them as a chasm of fear to fall into and more of an opportunity to spread your wings and soar!

"Far away there in the sunshine are my highest aspirations. I may not reach them, but I can look up and see their beauty, believe in them, and try to follow where they lead."
— Louisa May Alcott

12

FEAR AND SEPARATION:
BREAKING DOWN WALLS

"Every second, we choose to nourish ourselves in a way that supports or depletes our lives, and to think and speak about other people in a way that is honoring or dishonoring. What choice are you going to make today?"
— **Gregg Braden, author of** *The Divine Matrix*

The Ripple Effect

The Bible says that when Jesus hung on the cross, he looked upon his tormentors and blessed them saying, "Father, forgive them for they know not what they do." He understood the power the fear-mind has over people. He had every reason righteously to take on the victim role. The gospels say he had the power of the Hosts of Heaven at his command, yet his focus was not revenge, but one of empathy toward his abusers.

Chester likes to be "the man." When he is identified and "busted," his ability to be the imposter is taken away. When ego is king, the only possible response to injustice is more and often greater injustice and retaliation and pain.

"Peace is not achieved by controlling nations,
but mastering our thoughts."
— **John Harricharan**

We have an opportunity to soar in life rather than grovel in the dirt as victims, but if we identify with the commonly held belief of fear portrayed by the world, we are in danger of being victims.

Our country is now many years and thousands of lives into a conflict that is a perfect example of a classic fear-based response. Injustice was served to us, and more pain in kind was returned. Tragically, the expense of all this fear has been the loss of a tremendous number of human lives on both sides of the conflict.

Eckhart Tolle suggests that suffering is necessary only as long as we need to find an opportunity for conscious spiritual growth and healing. If the victim role is indeed false and an illusion, the only real role (personally, corporately, or nationally) any of us has is that of the co-creator. And therefore, suffering truly is a result of our own conditioned fear response. The pain felt is an opportunity to turn to inward reflection and spiritual growth. I believe we (personally and globally) are on a path of accountability and true enlightenment. A huge window of opportunity has now opened for the human race, but it is not the only choice. There are other paths, even those that may lead to our destruction and extinction.

In *The Divine Matrix*, Gregg Braden expresses his belief that all things, spiritually and physically, are interconnected, and the connection exists at a level and depth beyond our feeble understanding of time and space. Braden proposes that every thought and action has an instant effect on each expression of intelligence in the universe. Science is just now beginning to understand and research this theory of a ripple effect. Studies and experiments in non-local phenomena and quantum physics support this idea and daily continue to uncover the limits of Einsteinian and Newtonian physics.

If all that is expressed is interconnected, what does it mean to me personally? If one thought of mine, positive or negative, does indeed instantly affect all of creation, indeed the entire universe, what level of accountability is that? And, what an opportunity to BE the Solution to the problem of fear and pain in my universe!

With this level of accountability comes the understanding that I really can never enjoy the luxury of living as an island, or disconnected. My every thought creates my universe from moment to moment, not just in theory, but in "real" ways! Because everything is interconnected, that provides me all the more responsibility and the more reason to understand, observe, and therefore, constrain my dear Chester.

The illusion of separateness is, without a doubt, the greatest impediment to global progression on the path of spiritual growth and enlightenment. This belief is the "anti-Christ" if you will of consciousness and spiritual maturity.

How long will we individually participate, or collectively as a race, in the B.S. (belief system) of separateness? How long will we continue to suffer in fear? Apparently, as long as it takes.

So many people are caught up in a flurry of effort to "fix" the condition of "the other." This is the basis of religion, of many political ideologies and most belief systems. If we can only convince others to believe the way we do, how much better the world would be! Then the planet could get back on track! If my belief is "right," is it not my duty to share my belief and expose the ignorance of my neighbor?

Most of the wars and suffering in history have been the result of one well-intentioned group of people forcing their "enlightenment" on another! Whether it is capitalism over communism, Christianity over paganism, the result is always the same. Further separation of people and with it any possibility of understanding and peace.

If enforcing my "gospel" on another is not the answer, then what is? How can my poor clueless neighbor get a "clue" unless I pull him out of his hapless, ignorant condition? Is it possible the whole paradigm of belief in a personal position is itself the error? If so, then how in hell (or heaven) do we save the world?

By leaving it alone.

In the movie, *The Horse Whisperer*, Robert Redford played a soft-spoken rancher given the task to rehabilitate a profoundly injured horse (and owner it turned out). The horse's emotional injuries manifested themselves in a high degree of violent behavior that would typically have been beaten into submission, or even result in the "putting down" of the animal.

The answer turned out to be stillness. Non-reactivity. No direct level of engagement other than Presence. I recall the scene where Redford's character just sat still for many hours until finally the horse had calmed and walked up to him in acceptance and submission. Eventually through example and mutual trust, a bond was developed that ultimately led to healing.

Ego engages and tries to force beliefs. Spirit allows. It truly is that simple. Not easy, but simple. Easy is furthest away when your personal Chester is allowed to engage. So disengage and allow. Observe and be still. Of course, staying still is pure torture for poor Chester, but don't worry, he/we will survive! Chester will do his best to convince you of the folly of "just sitting there." How is any "good" going to get done by doing nothing? If you just sit there, the "evil ones" will prevail! The terrorist will take advantage, torture the innocent, rape the undefended! All will be lost! Chester and his fear can be very convincing, especially when allowed to dominate our thoughts.

See fear as Chester's sword. If observed, Chester is not allowed to draw his sword. Fear surfaces when our attention is diverted. Watching the news, participating in fear-infused discussions with our friends, or a host of other opportunities will lead to the awakening of our dear Chester.

Fear of Separation

"Remember there's no such thing as a small act of kindness.
Every act creates a ripple with no logical end."
— Scott Adams

We are connected to the web of Life much like being a part of an immense three-dimensional spiderweb. I don't much like spiders, so this analogy has some built-in challenges for me, but if you can imagine a web that encompasses the universe and infiltrates and comprises all that is (and is not yet for that matter), you can understand the fallacy of separateness.

Every thought is perceived and transmitted throughout the web, much like the physical tremor in the spider's web that allows the spider to feel the fly's presence.

If we transmit fear and resistance through the web, we attract spiders of fear, trial, challenge, and opportunities to grow through suffering. If we vibrate and transmit love, allowing, acceptance, and joy, we are attracting harmony, support, and love from every corner of the universe!

The other paradigm is the belief of being separate. This is the doctrine of ego. This is Chester's world. Fear, distrust, anxiety, worry is the fuel for this paradigm. We perpetuate this way of living by feeding the fear. And there is Chester, fork and knife poised at the table, waiting, demanding to be fed!

How do you want to design your life? Would you like to experience joy, a quiet and confident peace? Are you tired of all the energy expended in worry, anger, and the feeling of impending doom?

What are you transmitting through the web? What scary spiders are you creating with your intention and expectation?

My personal understanding of and accountability for how things show up in my life took a huge turn for the better when I finally decided to agree with the Law of Attraction. When I finally saw that what I experienced was the result (sooner or later) of how I communicated with my universe, I fully realized it absolutely was up to me to create what I really wanted in my life.

This is the freedom for which we all search—the "peace that passes all understanding" of which the Bible speaks. As long as we point the finger, continuing to look outside of ourselves for the answers to our problems, we will continue to experience fear and pain and miss out on the "joy" that could be present in our lives. We will continue to attract the more difficult opportunities to learn, the opportunities that seldom feel good, but if resisted, will return, usually in a more intense form.

Many authors have written on the importance of remaining "centered" spiritually. For me, being "centered" means maintaining my connection with Source.

One cannot remain connected to Source while identified with Chester. Chester is centered in the belief of separateness, perpetuating a constant struggle to maintain a sense of self as an autonomous player in the big game of life.

In the end, we have a choice. We can choose to stay connected to Source, or we can choose to give into fear and allow ourselves to be separated. It is a constant struggle, but ultimately, it can be won as this old Cherokee story illustrates:

> One evening an old Cherokee told his grandson about a battle that goes on inside people.
> He said, "My son, the battle is between 'two wolves' inside us all. One is Evil. It is anger, envy, jealousy, sorrow, regret, greed, arrogance, self-pity, guilt, resentment, inferiority, lies, false pride, superiority, and ego. The other is Good. It is joy, peace, love, hope, serenity, humility, kindness, benevolence, empathy, generosity, truth, compassion, and faith."
> The grandson thought about it for a minute and then

asked his grandfather, "Which wolf wins?"

The old Cherokee simply replied, "The one you feed."

Five Steps to a Life of Joy

The word "Joy" somehow has acquired a connotation with a Pollyanna-like stigma. What I mean by joy is the ability to live your life free of the burden of fear. When released from the weight of fear, your daily life can be an experience of lightness, living on the verge of spontaneous laughter.

When I understood my Chester phenomena, I experienced a feeling in my life I had totally missed until that point. I could see Chester over in his corner, fuming in frustration and impotence. It was hard to feel sorry for the guy since he had caused so much trouble and grief in my life over the years. It was time for him to "chill" for a while.

My days were fun again. My relationships were a totally new experience. Gone was the expectation of imminent disaster. My joy created a vibration that initiated a series of attractions in my professional, business, and personal life that can only be described as a flood. I am still working at the art of achieving with what I could describe as an easy balance in my life. When you open the door of positive attraction, be ready to receive! And keep an eye on Chester! The little stinker will be waiting with his manual open and ready to dispense his art of sabotage. Chester wants a return to his "normal," and he will stop at nothing to return to his status quo.

Remember that Chester is you as well, but a "you" who, until this point in your life, has been out of control.

I have put together a few simple steps that will make it easier to maintain control over your Chester. Implementing the steps is simple; however, like any other discipline, it seems hard because it takes daily attention and not a little bit of focus.

Step One: Pause and create space.

The ability to place a momentary "cease-fire" on Chester's incessant noise and war-planning is a skill very few people possess. We can look at sages and wonder, "How do they maintain that quiet peacefulness?" It requires a consciousness and presence of mind that is not "of this world"—at least, not the world of the fear-mind, where Chester lives, communicates, and has helped to create and sustain.

To escape this fear-induced world, most people must create some type of crisis to stun Chester speechless. Very few people achieve this gift quietly and consciously, and how I envy those people who do! Their path looks easy from my perspective, even though in actuality, I am thankful for the path of learning I have created and I value each event and day of its unfolding. The pause does not have to arrive with crisis, yet that is the most common path we create.

"Keep your fears to yourself, but share your inspiration with others."

— Robert Louis Stevenson

Fear has a tremendous grip when given full power by our identification with ego/Chester. It typically will take a large amount of energy to break the bonds of fear identification and allow a window of consciousness to open up.

However it occurs, take the opportunity. See fear for what it is.

This brings us to….

Step Two: Observe.

Once the gap is opened, observe how your fear-mind welcomes the space.

You will likely notice that Chester must create some noise or a problem of some kind. Be ready for some drama. He must create something to fight against.

Chester is a bit of a vampire. His power evaporates in the light of observation and consciousness of Spirit. He delights in and grows strong in the darkness of unconsciousness. Ignorance is his shelter, and lack of oversight his playground.

The good news is that Chester is a pushover when he has been found out. He will become as harmless as a kitten when you are aware and watchful.

But beware. He is a sneaky little guy. A little neglect and he takes the advantage. A diversion of focus and attention and the kitten becomes a lion. How quickly and savagely our fear-mind identification can spring back to life, with only a slight "slip" in attention. A couple of days ago, my wife commented on how surprised she was at the suddenness of a fear/rage reaction when she was sure she had achieved control over her fear-initiated response. Apparently, we are never cured of the tendency, but with time, it becomes easier to maintain joy, and easier to "nip it in the bud" when it comes to Chester and his antics. Like alcoholics who are never totally free from the underlying addiction, our addiction to fear is very similar. "My name is Chester, and I am a fear-aholic…"

The condition may be terminal, but the joy of remission is wonderful! We can live a life in and of joy. Remember that joy is not something you find "out there"; it is resident in you. You are by definition joy in physical form. Remove the fear with your presence and observation and the joy that is you…IS!

The lesson here is that we must maintain the momentum of watchfulness on a daily basis—not a great amount of work, just a continual one. Observing may be the most difficult discipline to master. It becomes easier over time, but it must be continual.

Ego knows the charade is up the moment you shift from identity with form and assume identification with your Source. This gap, created by realizing you have the capability of observing, is the domain of miracles. It is also the place of conscious attraction of what you desire in your life. Unconscious attraction happens by default. Fear attracts that which will nurture and feed the ego with more fear. From the place of the observer, the light of your attention deactivates the fear machine. This is not a place of hard work. This is a place of joy, almost amusement at the silly games of the ego (Chester).

When your ego/Chester knows that YOU know, there is no going back and no place to hide. This is the fruit of the tree of "knowledge of good and evil." Once you take a bite of the fruit, understand the game, you will forever have knowledge of your fear's extent and your fear-identified self's capabilities.

How does one stay in the seat of the observer? How do you keep Chester on his stool, safe in his corner? It all comes down to choice. You have the opportunity (with consciousness) to select what enters your world. You either go into agreement with your outer environment, or you choose to maintain the integrity of your inner environment. You can swim in your own clean pool, or you can allow raw sewage to be dumped in it.

The books you read, the movies you watch, the news you listen to and choose emotionally to allow the activation of a response in you, the people with whom you associate—all of this determines how active Chester will be.

Step Three: Resonate

The space of pause and the awareness gained by observing gives the seeker of consciousness a platform of great strength. Yet this incredible place of opportunity can be forfeited in an instant with a fear-driven response. Revenge or even righteous defense absolutely negates the power of your conscious Self, and that's precisely why Chester will choose that path next. How can he do otherwise?

The ego craves action and reaction, especially action motivated by the fear response and designed to defend and build the sense of ego-identified self. When Chester pulls back his fear bow and selects his target, you need to be prepared—prepared to do what? Not to respond.

Rather than giving into the fear-mind, a far more conscious course of non-action is in the space of resonance and meditation. I am not speaking here of your typical sense of meditation, i.e. the lotus position, contemplating your navel and awaiting some magical enlightenment. What I am referring to is the space of communication and listening to the input of Spirit. You will be resonating, or vibrating if you will, with the energy of Creation itself. Ego must use force, thinking that it must drive opportunity, abundance, and creation into existence. Yet what the fear-mind most often creates is dis-harmony with Spirit rather than harmony.

I remember being seated in a circle at the retreat on Molokai. The warm fragrant breeze was floating in from the lanai and Bob was leading us in a meditation exercise. I was not a fan of meditation. My feeble attempts had only been met with intense fidgeting and discomfort. I now know that it was my fear-mind, Chester, fighting for his life, desperately trying to avoid the light of consciousness.

What I did not realize, what I didn't learn from Bob at the time was that meditation was not something that could be accomplished to any degree when Chester was in control. Now I understand that meditation is as simple as observing Chester. Meditation does not require hours of sitting rock still, incense, nor a Hawaiian setting.

Today I realize I can meditate at any time. What I call "walking meditation." Presence can be attained and Chester stilled with the simple act of awareness, of observation. When I arrived at this knowing, the hard "work" of meditation was over and the allowing of presence experienced.

Our work is to allow. To ask for, seek for what we want to draw into our lives. The manifesting of the items on our "shopping list" is the work and domain of Spirit. The more we engage ego to do the work best left to Source, the farther away we drive the desired result.

This state of resonance with Spirit is the domain of the Law of Attraction. We attract that with which we resonate. Some authors have stated that we create what we think about, and as the joke goes, if that were true, I would be a woman!

To control what we attract and resonate with, we need to calm ourselves, to be in touch with our Source. Meditation can be helpful with achieving this sense of calm. With my current understanding of the fear-mind, I can now see the value and usefulness of intentional meditation. With observance we can resonate with our Source and quiet the ego mind.

Once we achieve that quiet, we are better able to observe the thoughts that do arise. Thoughts are constantly in our thought-stream. We can observe them float on by harmlessly down the stream, OR we can fish them out, breathe them in, and then become emotionally attached and invested in their creation. Your passion and emotion are the catalyst for creation of your experience. Don't worry so much about your thoughts or become overly concerned that you allowed a negative one in; just stay in touch with your emotional response to a thought or stimulus—it is the emotional response that sets creation in motion.

Esther Hicks, in her presentation of the "Wisdom of Abraham," states that our emotional guidance system is an invaluable tool to use in the art of creation. Individually monitoring our thought-stream is not only exhausting, but time-consuming and a poor use of our attention. Some authors teach that constantly keeping positive thoughts in our window of intention is the way to achieving our goals. However, if you have tried using your will power to maintain "positive thoughts" constantly, you have most likely either been worn out or given up. Instead, our feelings allow us to realize when we need to search for a more positive thought.

The church taught me to distrust my feelings. This then resulted in the absolute distrust of the only trustworthy guidance system available to me! The confusion that followed took me many years to sort out. The disparity between my feelings and what I'd been led to believe were "the rules" was a huge gulf I could not then understand. I just learned to be suspect of my feelings.

If our feelings truly are our emotional guidance system, a system that was put in place to help us navigate this confusing world of thought and fear, then who or what do we trust? Do we place our trust in some church system, invented by human egos with varying and potentially harmful agendas and rules?

As a pilot, I learned to trust in my flight instruments. Not to trust them invites hazard and even death. So what do we trust?

Relax. Give yourself a break. Pause, observe, and then resonate with the vibrational level of the attraction you seek. If you vibrate low, with worry, exhausting mental exertion, or control, you will attract results in the lower vibrational spiritual realm. If you decide to vibrate with the higher energy levels of acceptance, joyous expectation, and allowing, your result will be high levels of vibrational return. It is a universal law.

Step Four: Receive

> *"Gratitude is not only the greatest of virtues*
> *but the parent of all others."*
> — **Cicero**

You may have noticed by now that a common theme in these "action" steps is a lack of action, or at least not the "active" action you would most often associate with making something happen in your life. But this lack of action is no mistake—it's the behavior that brings abundance and peace into your life. If you recall, the ego (namely Chester) loves the concept of creation through self-work. The fear-mind does not understand the Law of Attraction. That we partake in universal abundance by divine birthright is a concept foreign to ego. Chester is sure that with enough hard work, we can achieve a level of worthiness sufficient to receive.

The ego sees the passivity of receiving as weakness. Which of course supports the belief system (B.S.) of the fear-mind. Chester is a warrior who believes anything of value is earned only by force and effort. The Source-centered warrior understands that quietness is power, far more powerful than force. The way of the peaceful warrior is a discipline practiced by those who have chosen the place of the observer.

We have been sold a bill of goods. The errant concept that the universe is withholding reward and abundance is blocking our ability to receive—the concept that compensation must be earned, paid for, and worked for—is one of the saddest examples for ego-generated misinformation. We are by nature spiritual beings—spiritual entities experiencing the joy of physical expression. Spirit knows no lack. Scarcity is a concept of the physical dimension and a learned belief. The most enlightening and freeing accomplishment in this life is to unlearn our inherited belief of separateness from our spiritual source, the storehouse of all that exists and is available.

Like the layers of an incredibly thick onion, these belief systems can be peeled away to reveal the beauty of the innocent soul within. This innocence is not naivety, as the ego would have you believe, but an innocence strong in worthiness and knowing. Once you have reclaimed the knowledge of you and what you really are, you will have a level of spiritual security that is immune to the arrows of your ego.

"When you are grateful fear disappears and abundance appears."
— Anthony Robbins

To receive and to resonate with the abundant harmonics of the universe, you must be free from the interference of the "layers" built up over your lifetime. Ripping away the layers all at once can be very traumatic and painful, and in my observance is a fairly rare occurrence. The more common (and kind) method of personal transformation of Spirit is a gradual return of awareness and growing re-acquaintance of the Source-centered self.

Step Five: Nurture

No thing in our physical universe grows without care and nutrition. Your understanding of your spiritual essence (Self) is no different. What you feed yourself and the environment you nurture have a tremendous impact on your ability to resonate and receive the blessings of universal abundance.

My challenge is television. I appreciate the entertainment aspect of the medium; however, the tendency to receive an incredible amount of negative vibrational input in a very short period of time is a serious shortcoming.

When was the last time you took a good look at your immediate personal environment? What components make up your world? Is the music spiritually uplifting? Does it create a vibration that elevates your spirit or does it serve to excite Chester and his sense of fear-identified and enlarged self?

Many studies have shown that life forms, from plants to humans, respond to higher vibrational forms of environment. Music, plants, natural settings, or books that elevate consciousness all have a very great impact on the level of nurturing in your personal space.

So take a thorough look at your personal space. The home you live in, your cubicle at the office. What are you feeding your spirit? And more importantly, what can you do today to make a positive change in your own environment?

When you take the courage to step away from your fear-mind's response to external factors, you empower yourself to move through, beyond and above your fear. You are again in command of your life and your destiny.

After all, if you don't keep your space clean, who will?

13

THE WORLD AND FEAR

*"Nearly all men can stand adversity,
but if you want to test a man's character,
give him power."*
— **Abraham Lincoln**

Fear is deeply ingrained in our national and global consciousness. We treat our world neighbors much worse than we expect our small children to act on the playground. And we allow this behavior by our elected leaders.

"Suppose you were an idiot. And suppose you were a member of Congress. But I repeat myself."
— **Mark Twain**

We have much to be thankful for in our country. The solid principles of integrity, freedom, and tolerance that created the foundation for everything we hold dear continue to give us hope.

We also have much to be concerned about when we look at the current state of affairs around the world. Our leaders largely seem to have traded integrity for fear. Much of the "civilized" world now views us with dismay and distrust, if not outright disgust. Where once there was respect, now embarrassment all too often is the emotion evoked when the United States is mentioned abroad.

Marianne Williamson calls our world a "fallen world." I prefer to see it more as a disconnected world, identified more with fear than connected with Source. We have collectively bought into the belief that we are less than whole spiritually. This belief is manifested daily by fear-generated suffering around the globe.

I think Al Gore sums up well the United States' recent shortcomings in his book *The Assault on Reason* when he says:

> The Bush administration's objective of attempting to establish U.S. domination over any potential adversary was exactly what led to the hubristic, tragic miscalculation of the Iraq war—a painful misadventure marked by one disaster after another, based on one mistaken assumption after another. But the people who paid the price have

been the American men and women in uniform trapped over there and the Iraqis themselves.

President Bush offered a brief and halfhearted apology to the Arab world, but he should make amends to the American people for abandoning the Geneva Conventions and to the United States Army, Air Force, Navy, and Marine Corps for sending troops into harm's way while ignoring the best advice of their commanders.

Perhaps, most important of all, he owes an explanation to all of those men and women throughout our world who have held high the ideal of the United States as a shining goal to inspire in their land their own efforts to bring about justice and the rule of law.

Of course, a sincere apology requires an admission of error and a willingness to accept responsibility and to hold people accountable. President Bush seems to be not only unwilling to acknowledge error, but thus far has seemed unwilling to hold anyone in his administration accountable for the worst strategic and military miscalculations and mistakes in our entire history.

There was then, there is now, and there would always have been, regardless of what President Bush did, a threat of terrorism that we would have to deal with. But instead of making it better, he has made it worse. We are less safe because of his policy. He has created more anger and righteous indignation against us than any leader of our country in all the years of our existence as a nation.

He (Bush) has also pursued policies that have resulted in the deaths of thousands of innocent men, women, and children, all of it done in our name.... The unpleasant truth is that President Bush's failed policies in both Iraq and Afghanistan have made the world a far more dangerous place. It is unfortunate, but it is true.

How can the United States have moved so far from its founding ideals? Haven't we set ourselves apart in the world as the shining example of truth, freedom, and integrity? What kind of consciousness has led us to our current weakened position in the eyes of the world? At the risk of over-simplification, I believe it is fear and our identification with our fear-mind.

If I were to succumb to worry and fear, an easy reason would be out of fear for my children. I would fear for the world that we are handing to them. It is indeed embarrassing. Here we are, the grown-up folks, passing on to them a world infested with war, famine, and distrust. I know my own children are much more cynical than I ever was at their age. This state is absolutely pitiful and there really is no excuse, other than ignorance on a vast scale.

We know better. We teach our little ones in kindergarten better social skills than we exhibit in Washington, D.C. or around the world. We consistently react to and act out in fear.

Our country now has a new president. We have a new opportunity to be the change we profess we are. My prayer is that our new president will have the courage to make decisions in the light of Spirit rather than the darkness of fear.

The "hippy" generation of the '60s and '70s often thought peace could be obtained through angry resistance and demonstration. As the wars continued and we saw that fighting ignorance didn't work, many of us gave up. We became disillusioned with our world and settled back into the addiction of materialism.

It's time for us to "grow up" spiritually. To walk the talk. In *All I Really Need To Know I Learned In Kindergarten,* Robert Fulghum pokes fun at our insanity, wondering why we don't remember what we learned as children in relation to our current national issues—simple things like "clean up after yourself" (environment), "Practice the Golden Rule" (World relations), "Share with the other kids" (World economics), and "Don't take someone else's toys without their permission" (natural resources) all point to qualities that are very basic consciousness. I like Fulghum's idea. Let's just treat everyone like we ask our five year olds to treat each other. No big deal. Simple, right?

Now, I don't want to forget the millions of unsung heroes who do remember what they learned in kindergarten. Without them, it is likely we would have flushed ourselves down the cosmic toilet long ago. I applaud you. Thank you for Being when no one is watching.

Mother Teresa was once asked by a very successful businessman after one of her talks, "What can I do to assist in the change you are talking about? I have money; how much do you need?" Her response was very direct and simple. "I don't need your money. What you can do is go out into the street early tomorrow morning, find someone who is convinced they are alone and assure them they are not."

We change our world one person at a time. But the most important and the first person to change is "me." Maybe we cannot fight the darkness, but as individuals, we can each shine a bright light of consciousness out into the world.

My task is to shine my light of awareness into the world's dark corners and to hand my children and their children the cleanest planet I can. This is not an overwhelming task if I focus on my own backyard. To make a global change will require your help.

*"I see now that all creatures have perfect Enlightenment—
but they do not yet know it."*
— **Buddha**

We live in a very unique time. Science and technology dazzle us on a daily basis with products and concepts promising to make our lives easier, more productive, and healthier.

We continue to elect leaders who promise us a return to "a simpler time," a return to some form of sanity. Yet we continue to experience wars, famine, and cruelty that stagger any conscious mind. I hesitate to open my e-mail folder or glance at the Internet news headlines. Mostly I try to avoid them; however, every now and again I slip up and look. The media seems hell bent on providing every morsel of sensational negativity it can scoop out of the sewers.

And then serendipitously, a window of Spirit opens up. Recently, I watched a PBS special celebrating the ninetieth birthday of Pete Seeger, author, peace advocate, and musician. Performer after performer on the program graced the stage with old folk favorites in song and verse. Most of these people were from the Woodstock, Vietnam, and Berkeley era of decades ago—a time when we questioned authority, demanded peace, and truly expected our government would see the wisdom of spiritual consciousness rather than the insanity of egoistic fear-based actions and policies. But apparently we collectively had much more to learn the hard way.

Somehow, we elected more leaders the likes of George W. Bush, who with his cronies such as Cheney and Rumsfeld, all with the collective spiritual maturity of peanuts, proceeded to alienate the world. Our political hubris created a world that is now almost devoid of common sense, at least from a conscious standpoint. And what is truly baffling—these characters would be (and are) genuinely mystified when confronted with the destructive results of their "doing good."

But have we collectively learned any better? What do we teach our own children? Are the tools used in our parenting composed of spiritual integrity? Or do we defend our sense of entitlement?

We have "progressed" through the insanity of Iraq (twice), Afghanistan, and now flirt with the potential firestorm of Iran and other countries in the Muslim world. We continue to pontificate on what we see as superior moral stances while continuing to denigrate peoples and cultures much older than our own. We blame entire cultures of radical thoughts and practices without apparently seeing the hypocrisy of our actions.

We seem to be passengers in a car hurtling toward a cliff. Guess who is driving? Chester! That goofball!

Our fear-mind, individual and collective, seems to be out of control. We respond to fear with more fear, anger with more anger and violence with even greater violence. With each cycle, the pain gets deeper and more widespread. It may seem hopeless, but all we have to do is stop! Stop thinking! Cease giving all control to Chester and others in his position. Use the tool and then put it down. This seems very simple, but much harder to do in practice.

We have to practice moving away from the addiction to feeling entitled to our view of justice. When shoved aside in traffic or in the grocery store line, can we let our ego sit quietly on his stool in the corner? Or must we defend our little self and create not only misery for the other, but more importantly, for ourselves!

The news sources are filled with stories of seemingly normal, well-behaved people suddenly going over the edge, committing suicide, or going on murderous rampages for no apparent reason. What is going on? What could drive a mild-mannered father, schoolteacher, or factory worker suddenly just to "flip out"?

Something within is creating an insurmountable incongruence. Something is not adding up. The pain within cannot be suppressed by the apparent peace on the surface. The promise of fulfillment outside of our self is found to be illusory. The ego perceives this as tragedy and hence the ongoing suffering and pain.

We live in very interesting times. I cannot turn on the radio or television, or open a newspaper without being inundated with the negative outpouring of bad news. Violence, greed, death, and corruption seem to be the norm. Good news, if there is any, is typically put on the back page, if it makes the news at all.

Where does this incessant need to wallow in ugliness come from? How is it that with all that is beautiful and inspiring in the world, all we hear about is the crisis, not the miracle?

Chester feeds on fear. Our thinking mind responds to and perpetuates the problem and the misery. Greed for money and power consume the "consciousness" (or more accurately, the lack of consciousness) of the vast majority of the people of this world.

Chester is lost in the silent knowing of true power. Not force, but power. The "power" that ego understands must dominate and control, subjugate, and eventually destroy.

In the United States, we are reaping today the results of our past decisions and policies as a nation. I just finished reading *The Secret History of the American Empire* by John Perkins. A very sobering book. I could not put it down. For any of us to have an impact on re-creating the world we envision, we must accept responsibility for our part in this ongoing dance of fear. For decades we have manipulated, misled, lied, and abused as a nation. It can certainly be argued that we have done much good as well, but our avarice has unquestionably done immense harm. To blame the "other," to blame terrorists, or those with differing political ideologies, is to escape accountability. Even to blame our own political leaders is to miss the point. We, corporately and individually, are accountable. And with this accountability comes the seeds of opportunity for the change that this world must experience for humanity to survive. Not for the world to survive, but for us to continue to exist.

We (humankind) do not "need" to survive—although it would be nice! This life has its times of exhilarating, fulfilling, marvelous experience. But our existence does not have to be. Another recent book I appreciate is *The World Without Us* by Alan Weisman. At first I was offended by the very title of this book and resisted reading it, but once I did read it, I was enlightened regarding the (often very negative) impact of the "infestation" of human life on our planet—an impact that could have gone much differently. We have used force and greed to strip this earth of its resources, many of which are vital to its very viability as a living organism. Continued abuse of our resources may bring irretrievable and fatal harm to us and our global home in the very near future. Many experts feel that as a result of our actions, we are on the brink of no return from irreparable harm to ourselves and coming generations.

Life will continue to progress and express itself in the universe, even if humanity chooses to extinguish itself. Our opportunity is to transform this human experiment into the next phase of spiritual progression. This could be a world filled with people who appreciate, support, and learn from one another. We can create a world that uses responsible stewardship in utilizing resources for the advancement of life, rather than the oppression and elimination of life.

We can learn to love rather than conquer. We can choose to support and nurture rather than dominate as a response to irrational fear. What this will require is a level of spiritual maturity that is lost, sadly, on the majority of the world.

I like to believe that the tide of spiritual maturity is turning—that those choosing to ascend into consciousness are increasing in number and influence. I personally think and feel that the scales are balanced in the middle. Things could go either way for us.

What will your choice be when given the opportunity to awaken or roll over into that blissful slumber of subconsciousness? Will you help lean the scales in the direction of Life or darkness for humanity? Like in the movie *Star Wars,* we can choose to align either with the "dark side" (unconsciousness) or the "the force" (spiritual awakening and consciousness). Choose the force, Luke!

SECTION

4

VISION

14

LIVING BEYOND FEAR

"Our greatest glory is not in never falling, but in rising every time we fall."
— **Confucius**

What inspires you? If you were to wake up tomorrow morning and have the dream life you've always desired, where would you go? How would you spend your day?

I doubt you would spend your day at the mall buying more of what you really don't need. Would your day involve people? Relationships? Experiences? New locations?

My friend Bob gave me an exercise years ago I'd like to suggest to you. For thirty days, when you first wake in the morning, write down the first thing that comes into your consciousness. Don't think about it, analyze it, or label it right or wrong. Just write it down. Then at the end of thirty days, look at your list. Put together and coordinate common threads, thoughts, and desires. By using this process myself, it became clear that my inspirational mind, freed from fear and the "I should's" and obligations taken on by Chester, had a very clear knowing of what I wanted.

I challenge you to ask for and expect what you want in this life. If you know you are the creator of your earthly experience AND you have the power and self-appointed mandate to realize that creation, why are you doing anything less?

Move forward and through your fear. Observe Chester and his silly games. Appreciate his presence in your life. Know that the damage done by an unattended ego is not the end of the world. Know that with attention and intention, you can change from your current picture to fulfilling your life dreams.

Remember the joy you feel when you extend yourself in true joy-generated service to another? What would your life be like if that joy were the constant, the background that was the foundation for your moment-to-moment existence? I can imagine what your life would be like!

One of my coaches reminded me that we will navigate to one of two groups in life. We will either play the part as "player" of the game or as "maker" of the game. Essentially, if you are not creating your game, then by default, you will be playing someone else's.

It is a real "eye-opener" to wake up and realize we are pawns in someone else's game. To find out we have been following someone else's idea of happiness, someone else's idea of the "right" job, church, or place to live. To be handed the gift of coming to this realization is powerful, but also very sobering.

However it arrives, the empowerment that comes with taking ownership of what shows up in your life is incredible. The vistas and horizons you can see and experience when you decide to spread your wings are tremendous! For me, to be lifted on the currents of life and soar is worth all the stumbling and pain that brought me to that point.

Expect It All!

"Abundance is the way of the creative force in the Universe."
— Wayne Dyer

"Expect less and you won't be disappointed." Or so the saying goes.

That just doesn't work for me. I want it all. Fun, joy, incredible friendships, flying lots of helicopters….Why should we be content to settle for anything less than the absolute fulfillment of our wildest dreams?

Chester is whispering to me, "You're getting a little big for your britches there, buddy. Who do you think you are? Aren't you being selfish again?"

I have learned that there is no virtue in lack. Just as there is no salvation in excess. We have volunteered to experience this world for the experience and the self-expression it allows. But if we just sit here on our righteous, miserable asses, who does it benefit?

The church seems to be really good at instilling guilt at any inkling of personal gain. Somehow poverty has become equated with some kind of righteousness. Where did that belief come from? Let's take a real close look at that belief system. Seems like a real good way to control people. The ole' mushroom scenario, "feed 'em and keep 'em in the dark" philosophy….The fallacy that we need to be saved and that our joy and fulfillment is only in some far off heaven only destroys our ability to appreciate this heaven we have created. When we buy into these ideas, whether from religion or the people around us, we severely limit our chance at happiness.

I chuckle at the opening lines in the film *The Jerk*. Steve Martin plays a down and out bum, telling his story. He begins his tale with the line "I was born, a poor black child..." The movie goes on to portray, in a comical way of course, a perfect example of how far belief systems can go. Navin was born in poverty, told, "Don't trust whitey," and that he must be content with "who he was." But he wasn't "smart enough" to enter into agreement with what he was told and given. He wanted more. And he moved on to find it. And lose it as well, the point being that his mission was to explore the world and experience his dreams.

Like Steve Martin's character, we shouldn't be "smart enough" to buy into that way of thinking. Be Self-ish! Only by being personally healthy can we be the best for those we love.

I don't "need" anything, but I "want" it all. Need suggests lack and a universe that is less than abundant. "Wanting" is an activity that has been accused of being selfish, egocentric, and the old crazy falsehood that for me to get what I want, someone else must go without.

Because money has been equated with arrogance, abuse, and excess, most of us have a belief system about money and abundance that has created a wall separating us from the universe's generosity. That way of thinking is just plain FEAR! The belief that there is not enough to go around is at the root of misery on a global scale.

You don't have to continue to believe this way. The empowering step of choosing not to accept this belief system can set you free! Go for it! Dare to want! Dare to fulfill your dearest dreams, visions, and goals! If you choose to see the world as an abundant place, you will experience abundance. If you see lack, you will experience poverty. That is the law. That is how the universe works.

To understand how the universe is abundant and how we can experience that abundance, I recommend reading *The Law of Attraction* by Esther and Jerry Hicks. The book does a tremendous job in explaining how the law works, why and how we will attract by default that which we focus on, good and "bad."

By moving farther away from the crippling spiritual effects of fear, we will be able to see the possibilities of living a life of intention and abundance. But like all life processes, it takes focus.

We are universal travelers blessed with a brief journey here in physical form. We can respond to the urgings of Spirit to awaken to know our identity, or we can choose (somewhat painfully) to sleep the night through. As you look around, you sense and see the fear and its manifestations and wonder, "How is it that people can go on and not see?" You can understand the tears of Jesus as he paused astride the donkey at the gates of Jerusalem. He could see, sense, feel the ignorance, the unconsciousness, the fear that permeated mankind. The solution is so easily available, yet often so unattainable while under the control of ego.

Now that you aware, you have a choice. You can live free!

Identifying What You Want and Finding Your Purpose

So to move forward in joy your next step is to identify what you want.

I remember repeatedly being asked, "What do you want?" by Bob Trask while in retreat on Molokai. I was so confused and controlled by fear that I did not have an answer. I was afraid even to think that way. What do you mean, "What do I want"? Shouldn't the only thing I should want be "to know Jesus" and to "go to Heaven"?

After thinking about it and getting past my church-conditioned mind-set, I did know I wanted something more than just "things." I was starving for purpose.

I have since come to understand that my life's purpose is to share by word and example the value of moving beyond the pain of spiritual unconsciousness. Consciousness is always preferable to unconsciousness. To help others reclaim the knowledge that we are spiritual beings having a physical experience is my true life's work. It is my purpose to share this understanding with as many people as possible while I am on this earth in this physical form.

I realized early on in my spiritual journey that there was no going back. As painful as awakening is, as uncomfortable as the journey can be at times, and as inviting as sleep appears, when I am quiet and reflect, I know all is well. I KNOW it is all worth the journey. Life is indeed a sweet gift. This knowing brings with it the gratitude that eases the pain and smoothes the bumps and jolts of the path chosen.

"As we express our gratitude, we must never forget that the highest appreciation is not to utter words, but to live by them."
— John Fitzgerald Kennedy

I know that after reading this book, there is no going back for you either! Thanks a lot, right? You may be muttering all manner of choice words under your breath in my direction just now, but to know what fear is, to know how it has crippled your experience to this point, I know it is worth it to you.

As your candle is lit, light another. Millions of people on this earth are looking in the wrong place for meaning in their lives. Too late, many are finding out that material accomplishment and gain is just not enough. That void in their souls cannot be filled with anything but Source.

Robert Fulghum, in his book *It Was On Fire When I Lay Down On It*, shares a story that is probably more precious to me than any other I have read or heard. A modern day Greek philosopher by the name of Alexander Papaderos was bringing to a close a seminar at his institute on the isle of Crete. This island had been the site of tremendous suffering during World War II, and his institute was dedicated to the shared goal of global peace and understanding. Fulghum shares this story of his experience in understanding his life's work:

> At the last session on the last morning of a two week seminar on Greek culture, led by intellectuals and experts in their fields who were recruited by Papaderos from across Greece, Papaderos rose from his chair at the back of the room and walked to the front, where he stood in the bright Greek sunlight of an open window and looked out. We followed his gaze across the bay to the iron cross marking the German cemetery.
>
> He turned. And made the ritual gesture: "Are there any questions?"

Quiet quilted the room. These two weeks had generated enough questions for a lifetime, but for now there was only silence.

"No questions?" Papaderos swept the room with his eyes.

So. I asked.

"Dr. Papaderos, what is the meaning of life?"

The usual laughter followed, and people stirred to go.

Papaderos held up his hand and stilled the room and looked at me for a long time, asking with his eyes if I was serious and seeing from my eyes that I was.

"I will answer your question."

Taking his wallet out of his hip pocket, he fished into a leather billfold and brought out a very small round mirror, about the size of a quarter.

And what he said went like this:

"When I was a small child, during the war, we were very poor and we lived in a remote village. One day, on the road, I found the broken pieces of a mirror. A German motorcycle had been wrecked in that place.

"I tried to find all the pieces and put them together, but it was not possible, so I kept only the largest piece. This one. And by scratching it on a stone I made it round. I began to play with it as a toy and became fascinated by the fact that I could reflect light into dark places where the sun would never shine—in deep holes and crevices and dark closets. It became a game for me to get light into the most inaccessible places I could find.

"I kept the little mirror, and as I went about my growing up, I would take it out in idle moments and continue the challenge of the game. As I became a man, I grew to understand that this was not just a child's game but a metaphor for what I might do with my life. I came to understand that I am not the light or the source of light. But light—truth, understanding, knowledge—is there, and it will only shine in many dark places if I reflect it.

"I am a fragment of a mirror whose whole design and shape I do not know. Nevertheless, with what I have I can reflect light into the dark places of this world—into the black places in the hearts of men—and change some things in some people. Perhaps others may see and do likewise. This is what I am about. This is the meaning of my life."

And then he took his small mirror and, holding it carefully, caught the bright rays of daylight streaming through the window and reflected them onto my face and onto my hands folded on the desk.

I love that analogy. Fulghum's story brings a lump to my throat each time I read it. My purpose is not to preach. Not to make anyone wrong. Not to imply that anyone is less than whole. My purpose is simply to reflect source into the heart of another.

I lost my evangelical zeal for religion many years ago. I remember when I was sure my purpose in life was to be a minister in my church. The essence of that knowing has not been lost—I am a minister, but the form of that purpose has changed. My purpose in life is to awaken and enlighten others. Not to my form of what is "right," but to help people see how much fear has obscured the light of their divine spirit. To recognize that they lack for nothing. That no church, dogma, sect, or person holds the truth or answer for them.

For the ego, that is all but impossible. Ego must "do." Ego must find an answer outside of self. Chester has to have a problem to solve. He must have something to strive toward, to attain. He cannot understand the words "You are complete now, and you always have been."

Each of us is sitting on our fortune. The answer to all of life's questions is no further away than a window of awareness. All we have to do is to allow that which already is. Most people will succumb to the path of least resistance. Until some inner incentive, or some crisis creates a window of opportunity, awareness will remain dormant. What is the key factor in stirring this awakening to the potential of life? Of consciousness? These are questions that continue to intrigue me. Why do some awaken while others do not? Why is one person content to sit in front of a slot machine, inhaling cigarette after cigarette, drink in the other hand, cursing his misfortune? Why does another person become inspired with the realization that he is an infinite soul, that he himself (or rather an awareness of self) is the key factor to a life of immeasurable possibility? I haven't figured that one out yet. Unless it is according to the old maxim, "The simplest solution is most likely the truest," that our life is preordained before our first breath. Not by some arbitrary guy with a white beard floating on some cloud "out there," but by our original, true, essential Self, intentionally drafting the syllabus and outline of our coming physical experience.

The latter resonates with me. We created our experience here to experience, express, and grow. Who is to say, other than our original Self, at what speed and how many lifetimes it takes for an opportunity of expression to unfold itself?

As I was sitting under the strawberry guava bush, high on a hillside on east Molokai, these and other questions floated through my mind like the clouds riding high on the trade winds above the islands. What is my life purpose? Does the path to "enlightenment," knowing, require tremendous effort by my egoistic mind/Chester? Does my problem-solving intellect need to nail down an absolutely scientific understanding of my life's path? Or is the greater spiritual wisdom as simple as assuming an attitude of allowing that places infinite trust in the same Wisdom that brought me into this physical being?

After many years and thousands of questions, many of them unanswered by anyone or anything outside of myself, what I have come to understand is the direct correlation between the degree of my egoistic effort and my resulting emotional and spiritual pain. The more I push, the more I create resistance, which is naturally followed by more pain. So I resolve to stop, or at least intentionally minimize, my pushing and therefore pain. The "Let go and let God" approach to navigating my life.

I have learned that meditation is not forced. My earliest attempts at meditation were exercises in frustrating futility. I've learned the key to successful meditation is to stop trying, stop pushing with my thinking mind, and simply to observe, and within the space of observing, allow. Eckhart Tolle illustrates this process by suggesting you imagine yourself as a cat watching a mouse hole, waiting for the mouse to emerge. With observance, you quickly discover that unnecessary thinking ceases. It takes a long time for any thought to pop up. By holding still the thinking, problem-solving mind, Chester's busy work is put on hold. Life begins to unfold with relative ease, and each moment is met by its answering solution. The peace "that passes all understanding" is realized.

"Your inner purpose is to awaken. It is as simple as that. You share that purpose with every other person on the planet—because it is the purpose of humanity. Your inner purpose is an essential part of the purpose of the whole. Your outer purpose can change over time. It varies greatly from person to person. Finding and living in alignment with the inner purpose is the foundation for fulfilling your outer purpose. It is the basis for true success."
— **Eckhart Tolle**

15

SOARING IN JOY

"Our deepest fear is not that we are inadequate. Our deepest fear is that we are powerful beyond measure. It is our light, not our darkness that most frightens us. We ask ourselves, Who am I to be brilliant, gorgeous, talented, fabulous? Actually, who are you not to be? You are a child of God. Your playing small does not serve the world. There is nothing enlightened about shrinking so that other people won't feel insecure around you. We are all meant to shine, as children do. We were born to make manifest the glory of God that is within us. It is not just in some of us; it is in everyone. And as we let our own light shine, we unconsciously give other people permission to do the same. As we are liberated from our won fear, our presence automatically liberates others."

— **Marianne Williamson,** *A Return to Love*

A few years ago, Bob Trask gave me another of those thirty day exercises. This time when I woke up each morning, the first thing I was to do was ask myself, "What would you do today if money were no object and you were free to do whatever you wanted?"

I kept the list for thirty days and was instructed to look down through the list and find the common thread. Before Chester woke up in the morning and interrupted me with his litany of fears and impossibilities, what central theme was shining through?

I challenge you to ask yourself the same question. What are you avoiding? And who do you think is benefiting from this crippling suppression of you living your life?

Go ahead. Take thirty days and make a list. Before your thinking mind interferes, find out what your spirit is trying to tell you. You owe it to yourself to find out!

My coach from years past, Dr. Mark Rademacher, used to tell me that we could have anything we wanted in this life. But we couldn't realistically have it all. If our intent is strong enough, our focus laser sharp, our commitment to the goal bigger than any obstacle, we can have whatever we want!

Now of course, no matter how badly I may want it, I'll probably not be the head ballerina for the ballet. Not saying that is what I want, don't get worried here; it's just that there are limitations of matter that we created when we chose to show up here. But we can attain what Chester would call impossible.

A favorite movie of mine is *Rudy*. Here is a guy, five foot nothing, not much of an athlete, not too smart apparently either. But he had an intention the size of Everest! He was going to play football for the Fighting Irish, Notre Dame. And nothing stood in his way for long.

This is the value of intent and passion. Passion, vision, and believing in your goal will keep Chester nailed to his stool. He thrives on drama, conflict, and energy draining diversions that pull us away from our source. Don't let him do it. Keep an eye on the guy. Like I've said before, the guy's a troublemaker.

When I wake up in the morning, if I'm smart, I have a little talk with myself. I make some intentions, some decisions for the day that set the stage for my success.

My goal for the day is not to create more difficulty in my life. I choose to see the limits of my fear-based mind, my Chester, and not let him hamper my showing up at life school. Learning experiences, sure, bring them on! That is what this life is all about. Learning and experiencing. Smelling the roses, tasting the peaches, and yes, being pricked by the thorns. The difficulty is our non-acceptance, our resistance to what WE have invited into our life for a purpose.

A Final Note of Caution

There is danger in giving Chester a little more credit than is his due. What I mean is that it can be very helpful to remember that Chester is a phantom, granted a sometimes quite scary apparition, but essentially of little substance nonetheless. He is an illusion despite all of the flurry and noise he so likes to create.

A puppet, no matter how life-like, is reduced to a thin pile of fabric, wooden sticks, and string when the animating presence is removed. Your participation in the drama of Chester is what gives him life and substance. With your presence and observation, this sustaining animation is removed and you no longer need to divide yourself and identify with this false imitation of self. You are again the divine One.

The danger is one of distraction and non-presence. Your Chester is counting on creating a gap between your presence and your attention. He will continue to look for opportunities to draw your attention back into the drama and fear. The good news is that as you become more aware, it will be become much easier to remain centered and keep this gap closed. There is no effort involved here, only your calm attention.

So enough of Chester. You can now place the puppet back on his shelf and decide to live a life of joy, presence, and love.

And don't take yourself too seriously. Remember that…

"There's nothing wrong with you that reincarnation won't cure."
— Jack E. Leonard

Let me close with this beautiful explanation of who you really are, by Rob Breszny:

You are one of the chosen ones.
You're a luminous being.
A primordial miracle. A resplendent avatar.
You are a deity in disguise—not a Buddha or a Christ, but of the same lineage and made from the same mojo.

I want to be sure you get what I'm saying.
You're an immortal messiah.
You have been around since the beginning of time and will be here after the end.
Every day and in every way, you're getting better at playing the mysterious master game we all dreamed up together before the Big Bang bloomed.

Let me put it another way.
You're a rebel creator longing to make the whole universe your home and sanctuary.
You are a dissident bodhisattva joyfully struggling to

germinate the seeds of divine love that are packed inside every moment.

It's time to remember.

You are a shimmering burst of spiral hallelujahs that has temporarily taken on the form of a human being, agreeing to endure amnesia about your true origins.

And why did you do that? Because it was the best way to forge the exquisitely unique and robust identity that would make you such an elemental force in our 14-billion-year campaign to bring heaven all the way down to earth.

You and I are freedom fighters scrambling and finagling and conspiring to relieve all of our fellow messiahs from their suffering and shower them with more blessings than they know what to do with.

— Rob Breszny

RECOMMENDED READING

Andrews, Andy. *Mastering the Seven Decisions That Determine Personal Success: An Owner's Manual to the New York Times Bestseller,* The Traveler's Gift. Nashville, TN: Thomas Nelson, 2008.

Braden, Gregg. *The Divine Matrix: Bridging Time, Space, Miracles, and Belief.* Carlsbad, CA: Hay House, 2008.

Castle, Victoria. *The Trance of Scarcity: Stop Holding Your Breath and Start Living Your Life.* San Francisco, CA: Berrett-Koehler Publishers, 2007.

Dyer, Wayne. *Manifest Your Destiny: The Nine Spiritual Principles for Getting Everything You Want.* New York, NY: HarperCollins Paperbacks, 1997.

Fulghum, Robert. *All I Really Need to Know I Learned in Kindergarten.* New York, NY: Ballantine Books, 2004.

Fulghum, Robert. *It Was On Fire When I Lay Down On It.* New York, NY: Random House, 1998.

Gore, Al. *The Assault on Reason*. New York, NY: Penguin, 2008.

Hawkins, David. *Power vs. Force: The Hidden Determinants of Human Behavior*. Carlsbad, CA: Hay House, 2002.

Hicks, Esther and Jerry. *The Law of Attraction: The Basics of the Teachings of Abraham*. Carlsbad, CA: Hay House, 2006.

Lipton, Bruce. *The Biology of Belief*. Carlsbad, CA: Hay House, 2008.

Perkins, John. *The Secret History of the American Empire: The Truth About Economic Hit Men, Jackals, and How to Change the World*. New York, NY: Plume, 2008.

Perkins, John. *Confessions of an Economic HitMan*. San Francisco, CA: Berrett-Koehler, 2005.

Phillips, Kevin. *Bad Money: Reckless Finance, Failed Politics, and the Global Crisis of American Capitalism*. New York, NY: Penguin, 2009.

Plasker, Eric. *The 100 Year Lifestyle: Dr. Plasker's Breakthrough Solution for Living Your Best Life—Every Day of Your Life!* Cincinnati, OH: Adams Media, 2007.

Ramo, Joshua Cooper. *The Age of the Unthinkable: Why the New World Disorder Constantly Surprises Us And What We Can Do About It*. New York, NY: Little, Brown and Company, 2009.

Ruiz, Don Miguel. *The Four Agreements: A Practical Guide to Personal Freedom.* San Rafael, CA: Amber-Allen, 1997.

Tolle, Eckhart. *The Power of Now: A Guide to Spiritual Enlightenment.* Novato, CA: New World Library, 2004.

Twist, Lynne. *The Soul of Money: Reclaiming the Wealth of Our Inner Resources.* New York, NY: W.W. Norton & Co., 2006.

Weisman, Alan. *The World Without Us.* New York, NY: Picador, 2008.

ABOUT THE AUTHOR

Perry L. Chinn has been a doctor of chiropractic for twenty-three years. In addition to successfully running a small business and practice, he is a success coach and writer, rotor wing instructor, nutritional product developer, and personal growth consultant.

Born in Idaho, Dr. Chinn has lived most of his life in the Pacific Northwest. He is married to Melanie Vizzutti Chinn, and he is the father of four boys and three stepdaughters, as well as being a proud grandfather. His other activities include hiking, cycling, traveling, and singing his tenth season as a tenor with the Seattle Symphony Chorale. He and his wife currently reside in Enumclaw, Washington.

You can learn more about Perry Chinn at his Web site www.SoaringBeyondFear.com